Sanjeev Ka

No Onion No Garlic

Recipes to Keep Life Simple

In association with Alyona Kapoor

Popular Prakashan

www.popularprakashan.com

Published by:
POPULAR PRAKASHAN PVT. LTD.
301, Mahalaxmi Chambers
22, Bhulabai Desai Road
Mumbai 400 026
for KHANA KHAZANA PUBLICATIONS PVT. LTD.

(4348)
ISBN: 978-81-7991-789-3

Design & Concept: Devaki Baukar
Illustrations: Devaki Baukar
Photography: Sumeet Ballal

Printed in India
Infinity Advertising Services Pvt. Ltd.
D – 4/2, Okhla Industrial Area
Phase-1, New Delhi 110020

Author's Note

The idea of writing a book on recipes without the use of onion and garlic took seed when the prices of these two ingredients started skyrocketing and numerous requests to create tasty recipes without using these two bulbs came pouring in. And I must say that the challenge was extremely exciting and one I could not resist taking up. There are many who think that food cooked without these two bulbs will be uninteresting, bland and not quite palatable. But the fact is completely contrary to this.

In India you will find pockets of people who just do not eat onion or garlic by choice. And there are the Jains, who are universally known to not eat these two aromatic ingredients as well as any other root vegetable, because their religion does not permit. Yet their food is immensely flavourful. During religious fasts too, people refrain from the use of onion and garlic. So cooking without onion and garlic is really not a big deal. But the point we wanted to prove was that even the dishes that rely on these two ingredients heavily for flavour and taste, can be made without them and that too without compromising the taste.

So we – my team and I – started work on this book. We compiled the recipes that we felt would be liked by most – some traditional and some popular recipes were converted to suit this theme and some we created afresh. All of them were tried out in our test kitchen until perfected so, all you need to do is to follow them blindly and enjoy the results which are as tasty can be.

Our motto is taste is paramount and so we substituted onion and garlic with ingredients which gave results that were just as good if not better. Each ingredient has its own share of nutrients, taste and flavour which when used properly will give you excellent results. It all depends on us to use them diligently to get the best out of them.

While Chilled Watermelon and Yogurt Smoothie will quench your thirst on a hot summer day, Jeera Rasam will soothe your throat on a winter evening. Have Dal Pakwan for your Sunday breakfast and perhaps start a weekday with Chutney Dosa. Pack Aloor Dum and parantha or Rajasthani Pulao with Chana for your office tiffin. Enjoy Farali Bhavnagri Mirchi, Arhar dal with Palak, Ghiya Raita and steamed rice with your family at dinner. Mishti Doi would serve as an ideal sweet ending to a satiating meal anytime any day.

All the recipes serve four portions, keeping in mind that they form part of a menu with other dishes. Whatever trepidation you might have about cooking without onion or garlic, I am sure you and your loved ones will be completely satisfied once you make a meal of these dishes.

Happy cooking!

Sanjeev Kapoor

Contents

Beverages and Soups

Kesar Elaichi Lassi	6
Dahi Shorba	7
Aam ka Panna	8
Badam Milk	11
Chilled Watermelon and Yogurt Smoothie	12
Kokum Sherbet	13
Jeera Rasam	14
Palak ka Shorba	15
Tamatar ka Shorba	16
Bhuni Makai ka Shorba	17
Koolith Saar	18

Snacks and Starters

Ajwain ke Pakode	21
Alu Vadi	22
Chutney Dosa	23
Matar Paneer Samosa	24
Aloo Tuk	25
Mixed Vegetable and Beet Cutlet	26
Farali Missal	27
Jain Pau Bhaji	28
Dal Pakwan	33

Main Course

Corn Methi Masala	34
Aloo Gobhi Methi	35
Bhein Palak	36
Ganthia Saag	37
Cabbage Foogath	38
Baingan, Shimla Mirch aur Tamatar ki Sabzi	39
Aloo Dahiwale	40
Bhindi Amchur	45
Farali Bhaunagri Mirchi	46
Gurwale Shalgam	47
Kaju Dhingri	48
Punjabi Chole	49
Chana and Jackfruit Sukke	50
Kasoori Methi Paneer	51
Rajasthani Bharwan Lauki	52
Methi Mangodi	55
Turai Sabzi	56

Rice and Breads

Makai Parantha 57
Jalpari Biryani 58
Palak Methi Thepla 59
Rajasthani Pulao with Chana Dal 60
Adai 61
Spinach and Carrot Rice 62
Kachche Papite ke Paranthe 67
Matar Wadiwale Chawal 68
Aloo aur Khumb Biryani 69
Mango Rice 70
Bhature 71
Masala Puri 72
Pindi Biryani 73

Accompaniments

Amla and Green Chilli Pickle 74
Arhar Dal with Palak 77
Tomato Chutney with Dates 78
Ghiya Raita 79
Daalia Chutney 80
Pomegranate Raita 81
Aam Pickle 82
Chickpea Salad 83
Panchratni Dal 84
Sindhi Kadhi 87
Fruit and Nut Salad 88
Ghughni 89
Dal Maharani 90
Kadipatta Chutney 91

Mithais

Jigarthanda 92
Chana Dal Kheer 93
Churma Laddoo 94
Kesar Bhaat 97
Mishti Doi 98

Annexure 99

Glossary 101

Measurements 103

Kesar Elaichi Lassi

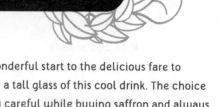

Cooling aperitifs such as this delectable lassi make for a wonderful start to the delicious fare to follow. Some people, however, like to end their meals with a tall glass of this cool drink. The choice is yours, a personal preference. One tip: you should be very careful while buying saffron and always look for the 'organic' label for there are a lot of adulterated stuff available in the market. Remember, buying saffron is almost like buying gold!

INGREDIENTS

A few strands of saffron

½ teaspoon green cardamom powder

4 cups yogurt, whisked

⅔ cup + 1 tablespoon warm milk

1 tablespoon rose syrup

10 tablespoons powdered sugar

A few ice cubes

4 pedas, crushed

4 tablespoons rabdi

10-12 almonds, slivered

10-12 pistachios, slivered

METHOD

1. Soak the saffron in one tablespoon of warm milk and set aside.
2. Combine the yogurt and the remaining warm milk in a bowl and blend with a hand blender.
3. Add the green cardamom powder, rose syrup and powdered sugar and blend some more.
4. Add the saffron milk and mix. Add the ice cubes and stir.
5. Pour into individual glasses, add crushed pedas and rabdi on top. Garnish with slivered almonds and pistachios and serve chilled.

Dahi Shorba

A medley of vegetables when cooked in a mixture of yogurt and gram flour add a new dimension to a simple soup. Assorted veggies not only make it colourful but extremely nutritious too. Whenever this soup is made at home, I don't need anything else to satisfy my hunger pangs.

INGREDIENTS

1 cup yogurt (dahi)

1 inch ginger

1-2 green chillies, chopped

2 teaspoons gram flour

¼ teaspoon sugar

Salt to taste

2 teaspoons ghee

1 teaspoon cumin seeds

1 medium carrot, chopped

5-6 French beans, chopped

1 medium green capsicum, chopped

2 tablespoons shelled green peas

5-6 small florets of cauliflower, chopped

METHOD

1. Grind the ginger and green chillies to a fine paste.

2. Whisk the yogurt with three cups of water. Add the gram flour, ginger-green chilli paste, sugar and salt and blend well.

3. Heat the ghee in a non-stick pan. Add the cumin seeds and when they begin to change colour, add the carrot, beans, capsicum, green peas and cauliflower. Stir well and sauté the vegetables for two to three minutes.

4. Add the yogurt mixture, stir and bring to a boil; lower the heat and simmer for eight to ten minutes or until it thickens to the desirable consistency.

5. Adjust the seasoning and serve hot.

Aam ka Panna

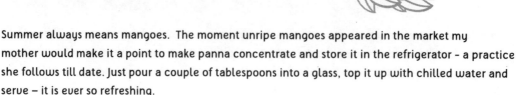

Summer always means mangoes. The moment unripe mangoes appeared in the market my mother would make it a point to make panna concentrate and store it in the refrigerator – a practice she follows till date. Just pour a couple of tablespoons into a glass, top it up with chilled water and serve – it is ever so refreshing.

INGREDIENTS

1 kilogram unripe green mangoes (keri)

4 teaspoons roasted cumin powder

2 teaspoons black salt

Salt to taste

3 cups sugar

METHOD

1. Wash and boil the mangoes. Let them cool. Peel, mash and strain the pulp.
2. Add five cups of water and mix well and cook till well blended.
3. Add the cumin powder, black salt, salt and sugar. Mix well till the sugar is dissolved. Cool down to room temperature and then chill in the refrigerator.
4. Pour into tall glasses as required and dilute with chilled water as per your taste.
5. Serve immediately.

Chef's Tip: You can dilute it with soda instead of water.

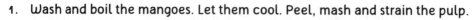

{Aam ka Panna}

{Badam Milk}

{Kokum Sherbet}

{Chilled Watermelon and Yogurt Smoothie}

Badam Milk

Badam or almonds are considered good for memory. I remember in our childhood my mother used to make us have a few almonds daily first thing in the morning. She would say it improves memory and thus helps us do well in school. And then the combination of almonds and milk is indeed very healthy.

INGREDIENTS

40 almonds (badam)

5 cups (1 litre) milk

A generous pinch of saffron

½ teaspoon green cardamom powder

A pinch of nutmeg powder

8 tablespoons sugar

METHOD

1. Soak the almonds in two cups of boiling water for five to ten minutes. Drain and peel them. Slice fifteen almonds and grind the rest to a paste.
2. Heat the milk in a deep non-stick pan over high heat. Once it comes to a boil, reduce heat to medium, add almond paste and simmer on low heat for fifteen to twenty minutes.
3. Add the saffron, cardamom powder and nutmeg powder and mix. Add the sugar and mix till it dissolves. Take the pan off the heat and pour into individual glasses.
4. Garnish with the sliced almonds and serve hot.

(Image on page 9)

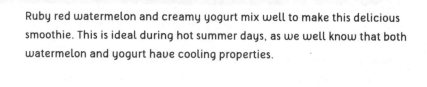

Chilled Watermelon and Yogurt Smoothie

Ruby red watermelon and creamy yogurt mix well to make this delicious smoothie. This is ideal during hot summer days, as we well know that both watermelon and yogurt have cooling properties.

INGREDIENTS

2 cups seedless watermelon chunks

1 cup yogurt

5-6 ice cubes, crushed

1 tablespoon honey

¼ cup chopped fresh mint

METHOD

1. Freeze the watermelon chunks in the freezer for three to four hours.
2. Blend the watermelon and yogurt with crushed ice and honey in a food processer
3. Stir in the mint leaves.
4. Serve chilled in individual glasses.

   (Image on page 10)

Kokum Sherbet

A healthy substitute for carbonated and caffeinated drinks…and kokum also aids digestion along with fighting acidity. You can replace the conventional pani in the pani puris (gol gappe) with this.

INGREDIENTS

100 grams kokum petals

¾ cup sugar

¼ teaspoon salt

½ teaspoon roasted cumin powder

METHOD

1. Heat three-fourth cup of water in a deep non-stick pan and add the sugar. Stir and when the mixture comes to a boil reduce heat to medium. Cook, stirring frequently, till you get a syrup of one-string consistency.

2. Meanwhile place the kokum in a mixer jar, add one-fourth cup of water and grind to make a purée. Add the purée to the sugar syrup and continue to boil for two to three minutes more.

3. Take the pan off the heat, add the salt and cumin powder. Mix well and set aside to cool down to room temperature.

4. While serving pour one-fourth cup of the kokum syrup into each glass, top it up with chilled water and stir to mix. Serve immediately.

Chef's Tip: It is an excellent remedy to treat a sun-stroke.

Note: To test if the sugar syrup has reached the one-string consistency, place a drop of the syrup between your thumb and forefinger and pull them apart. If the syrup forms a single string, it is ready. The scientific name of kokum is Garcinia indica and is also known as gamboge in English. Kokum is a native fruit of India and is grown abundantly in the Konkan region of Maharashtra, Karnataka and Kerala states along the western coast of India having adequate rainfall, good sunshine and fertile soil.

(Image on page 10)

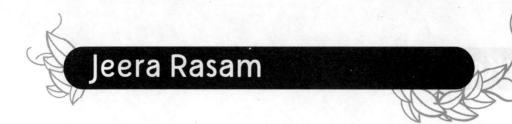

Jeera Rasam

The best thing about this rasam is that you can either have it as a soup or savour it with hot steaming rice. Either way it tastes just as good. I particularly like to sip on it when I have a sore throat. Try it; it is very soothing indeed.

INGREDIENTS

1 teaspoon cumin seeds (jeera)

2 teaspoons roasted cumin powder

4 tablespoons split pigeon peas, soaked

¾ teaspoon turmeric powder

2 medium tomatoes, chopped

Salt to taste

2 tablespoons Tamarind Pulp (page 100)

2 tablespoons rasam powder

¼ teaspoon asafoetida

4 tablespoons chopped fresh coriander

2 tablespoons pure ghee

5-6 curry leaves

1 teaspoon crushed black peppercorns

METHOD

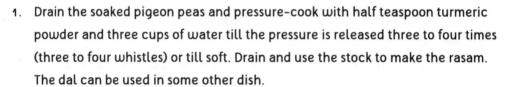

1. Drain the soaked pigeon peas and pressure-cook with half teaspoon turmeric powder and three cups of water till the pressure is released three to four times (three to four whistles) or till soft. Drain and use the stock to make the rasam. The dal can be used in some other dish.

2. Place the roasted cumin powder, tomatoes, remaining turmeric powder, salt, tamarind pulp, rasam powder and asafoetida in a deep non-stick pan.

3. Add four cups of water and boil for ten to fifteen minutes or till the liquid reduces to half of its original volume. Add the reserved stock along with the chopped coriander and boil for five minutes more.

4. Heat the ghee in a small non-stick pan. Add the cumin seeds. Once they start to change colour, add the curry leaves and black peppercorns. Add this spicy seasoning to the rasam and cover to trap the flavours.

5. Serve hot with steamed rice.

(Image on page 20)

Palak ka Shorba

Emerald green and full of taste, palak ka shorba does you a world of good. While cooking spinach one should be careful not to overcook it. Blanch in boiling water for two to three minutes, and then immediately dip in cold water so as to ensure that the bright green of spinach is retained. Overcooking will render the spinach black. Also salt it very lightly, for even a pinch more could make it quite unpalatable.

INGREDIENTS

500 grams fresh spinach (palak), blanched and puréed

2 tablespoons butter, at room temperature

3 black cardamoms

2 cloves

1 inch cinnamon

2 tablespoons refined flour

3 inch ginger, chopped

4-5 black peppercorns

4 bay leaves

Salt to taste

¼ teaspoon white pepper powder

1 teaspoon roasted cumin powder

METHOD

1. Heat the butter in a deep non-stick pan and when it melts add the cardamoms, cloves, cinnamon, refined flour and sauté for two to three minutes.

2. Add the ginger and continue to sauté for one minute.

3. Add the peppercorns, bay leaves, salt, white pepper powder, roasted cumin powder, five cups of water and stir. Allow it to boil on high heat. Lower the heat and simmer for ten minutes, stirring at regular intervals.

4. Take the pan off the heat and strain the stock into another deep non-stick pan. Add the spinach purée to the strained stock and mix well.

5. Place the pan on medium heat and cook for four to five minutes. Transfer into individual soup bowls and serve piping hot.

(Image on page 20)

15

Tamatar Ka Shorba

Tomato is a highly nutritious fruit but it is commonly used as a vegetable. This humble vegetable is highly sought after especially by health conscious as it is so rich in phyto-chemicals. What is more interesting is that tomato has more health-benefitting properties than an apple!

INGREDIENTS

12 medium tomatoes (tamatar), chopped

2 inches cinnamon stick

2 black cardamoms

1 tablespoon black peppercorns

2 tablespoons cumin seeds

4 dried red chillies

1 cup chopped fresh coriander stems

4-6 basil stems

2 teaspoons oil

1 teaspoon deghi mirch powder

4 tablespoons gram flour

1 tablespoon sugar

METHOD

1. Combine the tomatoes, cinnamon, cardamoms, peppercorns, cumin seeds, red chillies, coriander stems, basil stems, five cups of water and oil in a deep non-stick pan and boil for ten to twelve minutes.

2. Add the deghi mirch powder and mix. Take the pan off the heat and strain into another deep non-stick pan.

3. Add one cup water and boil it for five minutes.

4. Roast the gram flour in another non-stick pan for four to five minutes or till fragrant.

5. Add half a cup of water and one tablespoon of sugar and mix well.

6. Add this to the shorba and boil for five minutes. Serve hot.

Bhuni Makai Ka Soup

This is my sister's favourite soup. As a child she could slurp up this wonderfully-flavourful soup without any fuss. And my mother would be happy because makai or corn is nutrient-rich besides being ever so tasty. The initial roasting gives the soup a pronounced smoky flavour.

INGREDIENTS

2 cups corn kernels (makai)

2 tablespoons butter

2 medium green capsicums, roasted, peeled and chopped

4 cups Vegetable Stock (page 100)

Salt to taste

2 teaspoons lemon juice

2 teaspoons chopped fresh coriander

METHOD

1. Dry-roast the corn kernels in a non-stick pan for five to six minutes.
2. Heat the butter in a deep non-stick pan. Add the capsicums and sauté for two minutes.
3. Add the roasted corn kernels and sauté for three to four minutes.
4. Add the vegetable stock and salt and bring to a boil. Simmer for three to four minutes.
5. Take the pan off the heat and allow the contents to cool. Blend coarsely with a hand blender. Add the lemon juice, stir and bring the soup to a boil.
6. Serve hot garnished with the chopped coriander.

(Image on page 19)

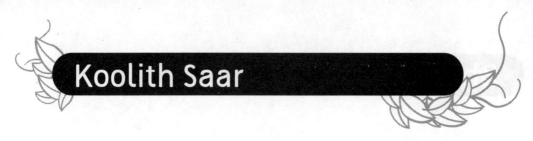

Koolith Saar

The first time I had it I was left wondering what it was made of. A Manglorean delicacy this, it is made with horse gram. Deep red and extremely potent it has a taste that lingers on.

INGREDIENTS

1 ½ cups horse gram (koolith)

2-3 dried red chillies

3 teaspoons Tamarind Pulp (page 100)

1 teaspoon coriander seeds

2 teaspoons grated jaggery

Salt to taste

1 tablespoon coconut oil

METHOD

1. Wash the gram and soak overnight in five cups of water. Drain and pressure-cook in 5 cups of water till the pressure is released four to five times (four to five whistles). Drain and use the stock to prepare the saar.

2. Place the red chillies, tamarind pulp, coriander seeds and handful of cooked gram in a mixer jar and grind to a smooth paste.
(Remaining cooked gram may be used to make ussal.)

3. Add the jaggery, salt and the prepared paste to the stock. Bring it to a boil.

4. Heat the coconut oil and add it to saar, stir well. Serve hot.

{Koolith Saar}

{Bhuni Makai Ka Soup}

{Palak ka Shorba}

{Jeera Rasam}

Ajwain Ke Pakode

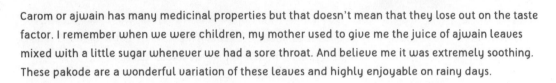

Carom or ajwain has many medicinal properties but that doesn't mean that they lose out on the taste factor. I remember when we were children, my mother used to give me the juice of ajwain leaves mixed with a little sugar whenever we had a sore throat. And believe me it was extremely soothing. These pakode are a wonderful variation of these leaves and highly enjoyable on rainy days.

INGREDIENTS

24 fresh carom leaves (ajwain ke patte), washed and wiped dry

1 cup gram flour

A pinch of asafoetida

¼ teaspoon turmeric powder

1 teaspoon red chilli powder

2 tablespoons rice flour

½ teaspoon Chaat Masala (page 99)

1 teaspoon carom seeds

Salt to taste

2 tablespoons oil + for deep-frying

METHOD

1. Mix the gram flour, asafoetida, turmeric powder, chilli powder, rice flour, chaat masala, carom seeds and salt in a bowl. Add two tablespoons of hot oil and sufficient water (about three-fourth cup) and whisk well to make a smooth batter. The batter should not be too thick.

2. Heat sufficient oil in a kadai. Dip the carom leaves, one by one, in the batter and deep-fry on medium heat till golden brown and crisp. Drain on absorbent paper.

3. Serve hot with tomato ketchup or green chutney.

Alu Vadi

This dish is made with slight variation in Maharashtra, Gujarat and Karnataka. This dish too can be had as a starter or as a snack or as an accompaniment to the main meal. Made with colocasia leaves which are covered with a spicy spread, it is first rolled and then steamed.

INGREDIENTS

12 colocasia leaves (alu che paan/arbi ke patte)
1½ cups gram flour
2 teaspoons coriander powder
1 teaspoon cumin powder
1 teaspoon red chilli powder
1 teaspoon turmeric powder
2 teaspoons sesame powder
Salt to taste
1 teaspoon green chilli paste
1 teaspoon ginger paste
4 tablespoons oil
2 tablespoons Tamarind Pulp (page 100)
100 grams grated jaggery
1 teaspoon mustard seeds
½ teaspoon asafoetida
¼ cup freshly grated coconut
4 tablespoons chopped fresh coriander

METHOD

1. Remove the thick stems from the colocasia leaves. Wash the leaves, wipe dry and set aside.
2. In a large bowl, mix together gram flour, coriander powder, cumin powder, chilli powder, turmeric powder, sesame powder, salt, green chilli paste, ginger paste, two tablespoons of oil and mix well.
3. Mix together the tamarind pulp and jaggery; add to the above mixture and mix to make a smooth paste.
4. Spread the paste evenly on the back of each leaf, fold over the two sides and then roll into a six-inch roll, making sure that all the batter is inside the leaf. Place the rolls on a greased stainless steel sieve.
5. Heat sufficient water in a steamer, place the sieve in it and steam for about thirty to forty minutes or till cooked. To check if the vadi are done insert a knife and if it comes out clean it is done.
6. Remove and let cool. Cut into one-fourth-inch thick pieces.
7. Heat the remaining oil in a non-stick kadai and add the mustard seeds. When they begin to splutter, add the asafoetida and put in the pieces and sauté till golden brown.
8. Serve hot, garnished with the coconut and chopped coriander.

Chutney Dosa

Dosa come in varied shapes and colours and this one is green. Absolutely enjoyable with dominating minty flavour, it is dosa and chutney rolled into one. The first time I made it was when we had some guests and since then we have them at least once a fortnight. They really do leave a lingering taste.

INGREDIENTS

1 ½ cups readymade dosa batter

1 cup roughly chopped mint

½ cup roughly chopped coriander

1 inch ginger, roughly chopped

2 green chillies, chopped

Black salt to taste

Salt to taste

Oil for shallow-frying

METHOD

1. Grind together the mint, coriander, ginger and green chillies to a thick and fine paste with sufficient water (about six tablespoons).
2. Add this to the dosa batter along with black salt, salt and mix well.
3. Heat a non-stick tawa. Pour a ladleful of batter and spread evenly. Drizzle oil and cook till underside is done. Fold into half and transfer onto a plate.
4. Serve hot with coconut chutney or ketchup.

Matar Paneer Samosa

Samose are a favourite snack of many. But if each time you get them with the same filling, it can become boring. I tried this combination once and it was a hit. Do try it and I can assure that not only will you love it but also whosoever you serve it will bless you for this delicious variation.

INGREDIENTS

Stuffing

½ cup green peas (matar), blanched

½ cup grated cottage cheese (paneer)

2 green chillies, chopped

½ inch ginger, roughly chopped

1 teaspoon cumin seeds

2 tablespoons chopped fresh coriander

Salt to taste

¼ teaspoon red chilli powder

½ teaspoon Chaat Masala (page 99)

½ teaspoon Garam Masala Powder (page 99)

4 tablespoons refined flour

Oil for deep-frying

Pastry

16 readymade samosa patti

METHOD

1. Put the peas in a blender jar. Add the green chillies, ginger, cumin seeds, chopped coriander and salt and grind coarsely. Add to the cottage cheese and mix. Add the chilli powder, chaat masala and garam masala powder and mix well.
2. Add four tablespoons water to the refined flour and mix well to make a thick paste.
3. Place a samosa patti on the table top, rub it lightly with the flour paste. Place a small portion of the cottage cheese mixture at one end and fold into a triangular samosa. Apply some flour paste on the edges and press gently to seal. Make the remaining samose in a similar way. Heat sufficient oil in a kadai.
4. Slide each samosa into hot oil and deep-fry on low heat till golden and crisp. Drain on absorbent paper.
5. Serve hot with tomato ketchup or green chutney.

(Image on page 31)

Aloo Tuk

One of the most popular Sindhi dishes – have them as starters, as snacks or as an accompaniment with sai bhaji, rice and sweet boondi. The best part of this delicacy is that it is so very easy to prepare. Just about anybody can make them to perfection.

INGREDIENTS

20-24 baby potatoes (aloo)

Oil for deep-frying

½ teaspoon red chilli powder

½ teaspoon dried mango powder

½ teaspoon coriander powder

½ teaspoon cumin powder

Salt to taste

METHOD

1. Heat three cups of water in a deep non-stick pan. When the water begins to a boil, add the potatoes and cook for fifteen minutes or till they are half cooked.
2. Take the pan off the heat and drain the potatoes in a colander. Allow them to cool and then press each between your palms to flatten them into thick discs.
3. Heat sufficient oil in a kadai. Deep-fry the potatoes till they are golden brown and crisp. Drain on absorbent paper.
4. Sprinkle the chilli powder, dried mango powder, coriander powder, cumin powder and salt and toss so that all the potatoes get coated with the spices.
5. Serve hot.

(Image on page 30)

Mixed Vegetable and Beet Cutlet

Anything fried is not healthy but if it is made healthy with vegetables it makes you feel a bit less guilty for devouring them. You just cannot stop yourself at one cutlet, you see. But maybe you can brush them with very little oil and cook them on a non-stick grill pan to sooth your conscience.

INGREDIENTS

5 medium potatoes, boiled, peeled and mashed
5 French beans, blanched and chopped
1 small green capsicum, finely chopped
1 medium carrot, grated
2 tablespoons shelled green peas, boiled and mashed
1 small beetroot, grated
Salt to taste
2 teaspoons ginger-green chilli paste
¼ cup cornflour
¼ cup chopped fresh coriander
2 tablespoons lemon juice
2 teaspoons Chaat Masala (page 99)
Oil for shallow-frying
½ cup breadcrumbs

METHOD

1. Place the mashed potatoes in a deep bowl. Add the French beans, capsicum, carrot and peas. Mix lightly. Add the beetroot, salt, ginger-green chilli paste, cornflour, chopped coriander, lemon juice and chaat masala and mix well.

2. Divide the mixture into equal portions and shape them into balls. Flatten the balls slightly.

3. Heat a non-stick tawa, pour a little oil on it. Roll the cutlets in breadcrumbs and place them on the hot tawa. Shallow-fry on medium heat, turning sides, till both the sides are evenly golden. Drain on absorbent paper.

4. Serve hot with tomato ketchup or mint chutney.

(Image on page 30)

Farali Missal

If you are fasting, I would suggest you have this for it is not only tasty, it is quite filling too. Alyona likes to have it during Navratri, when she fasts for nine days and it is but natural that she would like to have something different each day which is wholesome and tasty at the same time.

INGREDIENTS

4-5 large potatoes, boiled

2 tablespoons ghee

1 teaspoon cumin seeds

3 green chillies, chopped

1 inch ginger, chopped

1 teaspoon sugar

Sea salt to taste

¼ cup roasted peanuts

2 tablespoons crushed roasted peanuts

1 tablespoon chopped fresh coriander

½ cup batata chewda

METHOD

1. Cut the potatoes into half-inch pieces.
2. Heat the ghee in a non-stick pan and add the cumin seeds. When they begin to change colour, add the green chillies and ginger and sauté for thirty seconds.
3. Add the potatoes and toss. Add one and a half cups of water, sugar and salt and mix. Add the peanuts and crushed peanuts and continue to boil, mashing the potatoes slightly. Lower the heat and simmer till slightly thick.
4. Add half the chopped coriander and mix.
5. Transfer into a serving dish. Sprinkle the batata chewda and the remaining chopped coriander on top and serve immediately.

(Image on page 31)

Jain Pau Bhaji

Usually when you say pau bhaji you imagine a plateful of mixed vegetable bhaji with butter floating on top, garnished with a generous sprinkling of chopped onion. But what do the Jains do if they want to enjoy this delectable snack. Make them with unripe bananas and mark my word, you will find it just as enjoyable without potatoes, onions and garlic.

INGREDIENTS

4 medium unripe bananas

¼ cup shelled green peas

6 tablespoons butter

¼ small cauliflower, grated

1 tablespoon ginger paste

3-4 green chillies, finely chopped

6 medium tomatoes, finely chopped

4 tablespoons Pau Bhaji Masala (page 100)

1 medium green capsicum, finely chopped

Salt to taste

¼ cup chopped fresh coriander

8 pau

METHOD

1. Boil, cool, peel and mash the unripe bananas. Boil the green peas in salted water till soft, drain and mash lightly.

2. Heat three tablespoons of butter in a non-stick kadai; add the cauliflower and sauté for a minute. Add the mashed bananas and mix. Add the ginger paste, green chillies and tomatoes and mix. Add half a cup of water and cook on low heat for eight to ten minutes.

3. Stir in three tablespoons of pau bhaji masala. Cook for ten to fifteen minutes more.

4. Add the chopped capsicum, peas and salt and mix well. Add half the chopped coriander and one tablespoon butter.

5. Slit the pau. Heat the remaining butter on a tawa and spread the slit pau upside down on the hot tawa. Sprinkle some pau bhaji masala on the pau and toast on both sides.

6. Transfer the pau onto four plates and place some bhaji on the side. Sprinkle the remaining chopped coriander on the bhaji and serve immediately.

28

{Jain Pau Bhaji}

{Aloo Tuk}

{Mixed Vegetable and Beet Cutlet}

{Matar Paneer Samosa}

{Farali Missal}

{Dal Pakwan}

Dal Pakwan

Sindhis simply love to have this for breakfast especially on Sundays. Crisp puris with masaledar chana dal accompanied with a spicy mint chutney - ummmmm. Have this for your Sunday brunch and then gulp down a tall glass of malai lassi. After that a siesta is a must, for you will never be able to stop yourself from gorging on them. In the evening, make sure you go for long run.

INGREDIENTS

Dal

1 cup split Bengal gram (chana dal), soaked
Salt to taste
¼ teaspoon turmeric powder
½ teaspoon red chilli powder
¼ teaspoon Garam Masala Powder (page 99)
¾ teaspoon dried mango powder
3 tablespoons oil
1 teaspoon cumin seeds

4-5 green chillies, slit
8-10 curry leaves
½ cup chopped fresh coriander

Pakwan

1 cup refined flour
2 tablespoons whole-wheat flour
1 tablespoon semolina
¼ teaspoon cumin seeds
10-12 black peppercorns, crushed
2 tablespoons oil + for deep-frying
Salt to taste

METHOD

1. Drain the gram and pressure-cook along with salt and turmeric powder, half the chilli powder, half the garam masala powder, dried mango powder and three and a half cups of water till the pressure is released thrice (three whistles). Open the lid when the pressure is completely reduced.

2. Heat the oil in a small non-stick pan. Add the cumin seeds. When they begin to change colour, add the chillies, curry leaves, remaining garam masala powder and the remaining chilli powder. Stir and pour over the cooked gram, mix well and take the pan off the heat. Keep it covered.

3. To make the pakwan, sift the two flours into a large bowl. Add the semolina, cumin seeds, crushed peppercorns, two tablespoons of hot oil and salt. Add four tablespoons water and knead into a medium-soft dough.

4. Divide the dough into eight portions and roll each portion out into a disc of four-inch diameter. Prick lightly with a fork.

5. Heat sufficient oil in a kadai. Slide the pakwan, one by one, in hot oil and deep-fry on medium heat till crisp. Drain on absorbent paper and allow to cool.

6. Garnish the dal with the chopped coriander and serve with the Pakwan.

Corn Methi Masala

You will be surprised how with a minimal use of spices or condiments a dish can still be wonderfully tasty. If you find this difficult to digest, just make this dish. It is simple, but the best part of this dish is that you get distinct flavours of both methi and corn.

INGREDIENTS

1 ½ cups corn kernels, boiled and drained

1 medium bunch (350 grams) fresh fenugreek (methi), chopped and blanched

1 tablespoon oil

1 tablespoon ginger-green chilli paste

4 medium tomatoes, finely chopped

1 teaspoon Kashmiri red chilli powder

1 tablespoon coriander powder

Salt to taste

1 teaspoon dried mango powder

METHOD

1. Heat the oil in a non-stick pan; add the ginger-green chilli paste and tomatoes and cook till pulpy.

2. Add the chilli powder, coriander powder and salt and mix well.

3. Add the blanched fenugreek and drained corn kernels and cook, on medium heat, stirring frequently for three minutes.

4. Add half a cup of water, cover and cook for three minutes.

5. Sprinkle the dried mango powder and mix well.

6. Allow to heat through and serve immediately.

Aloo Gobhi Methi

This is the popular aloo gobhi with a difference and that is fresh methi. Cooked with minimum spices, it is something I savour because it sits light on my stomach. Goes fantastically well with phulke and Alyona packs this often for office tiffin.

INGREDIENTS

2 medium potatoes (aloo), cut into wedges without peeling

1 small cauliflower (gobhi), separated into florets

1 cup blanched, finely chopped fresh fenugreek (methi)

1 tablespoon oil

1 teaspoon cumin seeds

½ teaspoon asafoetida

1 inch ginger, cut into thin strips

1 green chilli, slit

½ teaspoon red chilli powder

1 teaspoon coriander powder

1 teaspoon Chaat Masala

(page 99)

Salt to taste

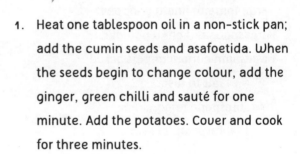

METHOD

1. Heat one tablespoon oil in a non-stick pan; add the cumin seeds and asafoetida. When the seeds begin to change colour, add the ginger, green chilli and sauté for one minute. Add the potatoes. Cover and cook for three minutes.

2. Add the cauliflower florets, sprinkle around two tablespoons of water and cook for five minutes.

3. Add the chilli powder, coriander powder, chaat masala, salt and fresh fenugreek. Mix well.

4. Cover and cook till the vegetables are cooked. Serve hot.

Bhein Palak

Lotus stems have to be cleaned thoroughly because a lot of mud gets entrapped in the crevices of the stem. Best way to clean them is under running water and by scrubbing continuously. That done you can cook in various ways. In this recipe we have added spinach which not only lends its green colour but also increases its nutrient value.

INGREDIENTS

150 grams lotus stems (bhein), peeled, boiled and sliced diagonally into thin strips

900 grams (2 large bunches) fresh spinach leaves (palak), blanched and drained

2-3 green chillies, chopped

3 tablespoons oil

½ teaspoon cumin seeds

1 large tomato, finely chopped

½ teaspoon red chilli powder

1 teaspoon coriander powder

Salt to taste

1 tablespoon lemon juice

4 tablespoons cream

METHOD

1. Grind the blanched spinach with the green chillies to a fine paste and transfer into a bowl.

2. Heat the oil in a non-stick pan and add the cumin seeds. When they begin to change colour, add the tomato and sauté for three minutes.

3. Add the chilli powder, coriander powder and mix. Add the sliced lotus stem and sauté till the oil separates.

4. Add the spinach purée and stir. Add salt and a little water if required. Cook till the mixture comes to a boil.

5. Add the lemon juice and stir.

6. Add the cream just before serving. Serve hot.

Ganthia Saag

This is just the dish to be cooked on days when you don't feel like spending hours toiling over the hot gas burners. It gets ready in a jiffy; after all the ganthia is available readymade. A favourite of the Jains.

INGREDIENTS

2 cups ganthia

1 ½ teaspoons red chilli powder

½ teaspoon Garam Masala Powder (page 99)

½ teaspoon dried mango powder

2 teaspoons coriander powder

2 tablespoons oil

1 teaspoon cumin seeds

¼ teaspoon asafoetida

1 teaspoon sugar

Salt to taste

1 tablespoon chopped fresh coriander

METHOD

1. Mix together the chilli powder, garam masala powder, dried mango powder and coriander powder in a bowl, add two cups of water and whisk well.

2. Heat the oil in a non-stick pan; add the cumin seeds and asafoetida. When the seeds begin to change colour, add the spiced water and bring to a boil.

3. Lower the heat and allow it to simmer for three to four minutes. Add the sugar and mix well. Add the ganthia, salt and stir. Cook for one to two minutes.

4. Garnish with the chopped coriander and serve hot.

(Image on page 42)

Cabbage Foogath

A lot of people get repelled by the odour given out when cabbage is cooking. But when cooked right it can be really delicious. Eat this simple cabbage dish with hot sambhar and rice and you will feel completely satiated. What's more, it is easy to digest, too.

INGREDIENTS

400 grams cabbage, finely shredded

2 tablespoons oil

1 teaspoon mustard seeds

8-10 curry leaves

2 green chillies, chopped

Salt to taste

1 cup freshly grated coconut

1 tablespoon lemon juice

1 tablespoon chopped fresh coriander

METHOD

1. Heat the oil in a non-stick kadai; add the mustard seeds and curry leaves. When the mustard seeds begin to splutter add the green chillies and sauté on high heat for one minute.

2. Add the cabbage and salt and mix well. Cover and cook, on low heat, for five to seven minutes or till the cabbage is cooked but still crunchy.

3. Add the coconut and lemon juice and mix well.

4. Garnish with the chopped coriander and serve hot.

   (Image on page 42)

This combination of brinjals, capsicums and tomatoes may sound odd to you but believe me it is absolutely fantastic. Try it out if you don't believe me and I am sure you will want to cook it very often. They go well with phulke or paranthe.

INGREDIENTS

8 medium brinjals (baingan), remove stems and cut into ½-inch cubes
2 medium green capsicums (Shimla mirch), cut into ½-inch cubes
5 medium tomatoes (tamatar), puréed
2 tablespoons oil
½ teaspoon carom seeds
2 teaspoons ginger-green chilli paste
¼ teaspoon turmeric powder
½ teaspoon red chilli powder
2 teaspoons coriander powder
1 teaspoon cumin powder
1 teaspoon sugar
Salt to taste
2 tablespoons chopped fresh coriander

METHOD

1. Heat the oil in a non-stick pan and add the carom seeds. When they begin to change colour, add the ginger-green chilli paste and sauté for thirty seconds.
2. Add the puréed tomatoes and sauté till the oil separates.
3. Add the turmeric powder, chilli powder, coriander powder, cumin powder, sugar and salt and sauté for one minute.
4. Add the brinjals, capsicums and sauté for four to five minutes.
5. Add one cup of water. Cover and cook on low heat for eight to ten minutes or till the vegetables are cooked. Serve hot garnished with the chopped coriander.

(Image on page 41)

Aloo Dahiwale

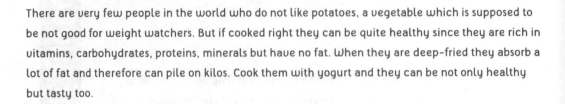

There are very few people in the world who do not like potatoes, a vegetable which is supposed to be not good for weight watchers. But if cooked right they can be quite healthy since they are rich in vitamins, carbohydrates, proteins, minerals but have no fat. When they are deep-fried they absorb a lot of fat and therefore can pile on kilos. Cook them with yogurt and they can be not only healthy but tasty too.

INGREDIENTS

4 medium potatoes (aloo), boiled, peeled and cut into ½-inch cubes

4 tablespoons yogurt (dahi), whisked

A pinch of asafoetida

Salt to taste

3 green chillies, broken into 3 pieces

1 teaspoon red chilli powder

A pinch of sugar

¼ teaspoon turmeric powder

1 teaspoon lemon juice

2 tablespoons oil

4 tablespoons chopped fresh coriander

1 teaspoon cumin seeds

METHOD

1. Add the salt, chilli powder, turmeric powder to the potatoes and mix well. Set aside for four to five minutes.
2. Heat the oil in a non-stick pan. Add the cumin seeds and when they begin to change colour, add the asafoetida, green chillies and sauté for one minute.
3. Add the potatoes and mix. Add two cups of water and mix. Add the sugar, salt and lemon juice and mix. Cover and simmer for five to six minutes.
4. Set aside to cool slightly. Add the yogurt and mix.
5. Garnish with the chopped coriander and serve.

{Baigan, Shimla Mirchi
aur Tamatar ki Sabzi}

{Aloo Dahiwale}

{Cabbage Foogath}

{Ganthia Saag}

{Kaju Dhingry}

{Gurwale Shalgam}

{Farali Bhavnagri Mirchi}

{Bhindi Amchur}

Bhindi Amchur

Amchur not only adds a delicate sourness but also flavours this ladies' finger sabzi. At home we prepare it at least once a week, as all of us simply love it, especially our younger daughter Kriti. Give it to her daily and she will devour it happily.

INGREDIENTS

400 grams ladies' fingers (bhindi)

2 teaspoons dried mango powder (amchur)

1 teaspoon turmeric powder

2 tablespoons coriander powder

Salt to taste

2 teaspoons fennel seeds, crushed

1 teaspoon garam masala powder

½ teaspoon red chilli powder

2 teaspoons cumin powder

2 teaspoons Chaat Masala (page 99)

2 tablespoons chopped fresh coriander

4 tablespoons oil

METHOD

1. Mix together the turmeric powder, coriander powder, salt, crushed fennel seeds, dried mango powder, garam masala powder, chilli powder, cumin powder, chaat masala and the chopped coriander in a bowl. Add half tablespoon oil and mix well.

2. Trim the tops and tails of the ladies' fingers. Make a slit on one side without cutting through and stuff the masala into the slits.

3. Heat the remaining oil in a non-stick pan. Add the stuffed ladies' fingers and cook on low heat, tossing at regular intervals, till almost done.

4. Sprinkle the remaining masala on top. Cover and cook for four to five minutes.

5. Uncover the pan and cook for five minutes more. Serve hot.

Farali Bhavnagri Mirchi

Plump emerald green chillies stuffed with a fragrant filling of sesame seeds, peanuts and water chestnut flour – simply irresistible. Actually these chillies are not very pungent. However, I still prefer to remove the seeds which further takes away whatever little pungency there might be. Cooked this way you can have them during fasting days.

INGREDIENTS

150 grams Bhavnagri chillies, slit and seeded

3 tablespoons oil

1 teaspoon sesame seeds

½ teaspoon cumin seeds

½ cup water chestnut flour

2 tablespoons peeled, roasted and crushed peanuts

½ tablespoon lemon juice

Rock salt to taste

METHOD

1. Heat one tablespoon oil in a non-stick pan. Add the sesame seeds and cumin seeds.

2. When the seeds begin to crackle, add the water chestnut flour and peanuts and sauté on low heat for two to three minutes till fragrant. Add the lemon juice and rock salt. Set aside to cool down to room temperature. Stuff small portions in the Bhavnagri chillies.

3. Heat the remaining oil in a non-stick kadai.

4. Add the stuffed Bhavnagri chillies and cook on low heat for six to eight minutes, stirring at regular intervals. Serve hot.

(Image on page 44)

Gurwale Shalgam

Shalgam in English is turnips and they are winter vegetables. In the north it is used widely to make the delicious gajar, gobhi, shalgam achaar. Besides having a distinct taste and flavour, shalgam is highly nutritive – low in saturated fat and cholesterol, it is a good source of vitamins and minerals and also fiber. This recipe uses jaggery to further the taste level.

INGREDIENTS

3 tablespoons grated jaggery (gur)

500 grams turnips (shalgam)

Salt to taste

½ teaspoon turmeric powder

3 tablespoons mustard oil

¼ teaspoon asafoetida

½ teaspoon carom seeds

1 tablespoon ginger paste

1 tablespoon red chilli powder

½ teaspoon cumin powder

¼ teaspoon Punjabi Garam Masala Powder (see page 100)

3½ tablespoons malt vinegar

3 green chillies, slit

1 inch ginger, cut into thin strips

METHOD

1. Peel the turnips and cut into cubes. Heat two cups of water in a deep non-stick pan and add half teaspoon of salt and a pinch of turmeric powder. Add the turnips and cook on low heat till done.

2. Heat the mustard oil in another non-stick pan till it begins to smoke. Add the asafoetida, carom seeds, ginger paste and sauté for thirty seconds.

3. Add the chilli powder, remaining turmeric powder, cumin powder, garam masala powder and jaggery and mix. Add the malt vinegar and mix.

4. Add the turnips and adjust the salt. Stir and add one cup of water. Cook for three to four minutes.

5. Serve hot garnished with the slit green chillies and ginger strips.

   (Image on page 43)

Kaju Dhingri

Want to make something shahi then this is the recipe for you. Cashew nuts not only add a richness to the gravy but also a delicious crunch. We make it very often when we have guests over and it is a great hit.

INGREDIENTS

½ cup whole cashew nuts (kaju), soaked

500 grams fresh button mushrooms (dhingri)

½ cup skimmed milk yogurt

1 tablespoon coriander powder

1 ½ teaspoons red chilli powder

1 teaspoon turmeric powder

1 tablespoon ghee

1 teaspoon cumin seeds

2 teaspoons green chilli-ginger paste

2 teaspoons black pepper powder

1 cup fresh tomato purée

Salt to taste

1 teaspoon Garam Masala Powder (page 99)

1 ½ tablespoon honey (optional)

1 tablespoon lemon juice

2 tablespoons chopped fresh coriander

METHOD

1. Remove the stalks of the mushrooms, clean and boil until three-fourth done. Drain and set aside.

2. Whisk together the yogurt, coriander powder, chilli powder and turmeric powder in a bowl.

3. Heat the ghee in a non-stick pan; add the cumin seeds and when they begin to change colour, add the green chilli-ginger paste and sauté for thirty seconds.

4. Add the pepper powder and sauté for two minutes. Add the mushrooms and continue to sauté for five minutes. Add the yogurt mixture and cook till the ghee separates. Add the tomato purée and salt and cook till the ghee separates again.

5. Add two and a half cups of water and bring to a boil; lower the heat and add the cashew nuts. Cover and simmer, stirring occasionally, for eight to ten minutes.

6. Sprinkle the garam masala powder and mix. Add the honey (if using) and lemon juice and mix well. Adjust the seasoning. Garnish with the chopped coriander and serve hot with rotis.

(Image on page 43)

Punjabi Chole

Usually onions and garlic dominate Punjabi cuisine but here we have made chole without these two bulbs. This is my mother's creation – she does not like the taste of garlic and is not too fond of onions. So she makes chole this way and we all enjoy it.

INGREDIENTS

1 cup chickpeas (kabuli chana/chole), soaked overnight ● 1 tablespoon tea leaves
Salt to taste ● 3 tablespoons oil ● 1 tablespoon cumin seeds
4–6 green chillies, slit ● 1 tablespoon green chilli-ginger paste
2 tablespoons coriander powder ● 2 tablespoons cumin powder
1½ teaspoons red chilli powder ● ½ teaspoon dried mango powder
● 1 tablespoon dried pomegranate seeds ●
1 teaspoon Garam Masala Powder (page 99) ● 2 medium tomatoes, quartered

METHOD

1. Tie the tea leaves in a piece of muslin to form a bundle (potli). Drain the chickpeas and transfer into a pressure cooker. Add six to eight cups water, salt and tea leaves bundle and cook under pressure till pressure is released five to six times or for twenty minutes or till the chickpeas are soft and completely cooked. Drain and reserve the cooking stock. Discard the bundle of tea leaves.
2. Heat two tablespoons of oil in a non-stick pan; add one teaspoon of cumin seeds, green chillies, green chilli-ginger paste, coriander powder, cumin powder, chilli powder and dried mango powder and sauté till fragrant. Add three cups of cooking stock and one cup of water and mix well.
3. Add the chickpeas and salt and cook on high heat.
4. Roast the remaining cumin seeds and dried pomegranate seeds till fragrant. Cool and crush. Add the crushed spices, garam masala powder and mix. Simmer till the gravy thickens.
5. Heat the remaining oil in another non-stick pan; add the tomatoes and sauté for two to three minutes. Adjust seasoning in the chole; add the tomatoes and simmer for two to three minutes. Serve hot with Bhature (page 71).

Chana and Jackfruit Sukke

This is a traditional dish from Karnataka, cooked on special occasions. I first tasted this at a Mangalorean wedding. I found the combination of brown gram with unripe jackfruit, blended with coconut masala simply amazing.

INGREDIENTS

1 cup brown Bengal gram (kala chana), soaked overnight

½ kg unripe jackfruit

3 tablespoons oil

Salt to taste

½ teaspoon mustard seeds

1 sprig curry leaves

A pinch of asafoetida

1 tablespoon grated jaggery

Masala Paste

1 tablespoon oil

1 teaspoon coriander seeds

½ teaspoon split black gram

¼ teaspoon fenugreek seeds

3-4 dried red chillies

1 cup grated coconut

1 tablespoon Tamarind Pulp
(page 100)

METHOD

1. Apply two teaspoons of oil to your palms and the knife. With the help of the knife remove the skin of the jackfruit and cut into one-inch pieces. Apply salt. Steam the jackfruit for five minutes. Remove from steamer and set aside.

2. Drain and pressure-cook the gram in two cups of water till the pressure is released four to five times (four to give whistles).

3. For the masala paste, heat one teaspoon of oil in a non-stick kadai. Add the coriander seeds, split black gram and fenugreek seeds and sauté till lightly browned. Add the red chillies and sauté for a minute. Grind to a coarse paste along with coconut, tamarind pulp and sufficient water.

4. Heat two tablespoons of oil in a non-stick kadai. Add the mustard seeds and curry leaves. When the seeds splutter, add the asafoetida and the ground masala. Stir well and cook for two minutes.

5. Add the cooked gram and stir well. Add the jackfruit pieces, jaggery and adjust salt. Stir and add half a cup of water. Simmer for five minutes, on low heat, stirring occasionally. Remove from heat and serve hot.

Note: If a steamer is not available, jackfruit pieces can be cooked in one cup of boiling water till soft.

Kasoori Methi Paneer

Dried fenugreek leaves or kasoori methi as it is also called, adds a wonderful smoky fragrance to any dish it is added to. However, here is a piece of advice – you don't add to any and every sabzi. But it combines fantastically with paneer to give a taste that will linger on and on and on...

INGREDIENTS

2 teaspoons dried fenugreek leaves (kasoori methi), roasted and crushed

200 grams cottage cheese (paneer), cut into ½-inch cubes

1 tablespoon oil

1 tablespoon green chilli-ginger paste

1 teaspoon cumin seeds

1 teaspoon Kashmiri red chilli powder

1 tablespoon coriander powder

Salt to taste

2 medium tomatoes, finely chopped

1 teaspoon dried mango powder

METHOD

1. Heat the oil in a non-stick pan; add the green chilli-ginger paste and cumin seeds and when they start to change colour, add the chilli powder, coriander powder and salt and mix.

2. Immediately add the dried fenugreek leaves and cook on medium heat, stirring frequently, for two to three minutes.

3. Add the tomatoes, stir and cook, over high heat, for two to three minutes. Add half a cup of water, reduce heat, cover and simmer for three to four minutes. Add the cottage cheese cubes, sprinkle the dried mango powder and mix well.

4. Cook till the cottage cheese cubes are fully coated with the masala and serve immediately.

(Image on page 53)

Rajasthani Bharwan Lauki

Lauki or bottle gourd is a less loved vegetable. As children we too were not too fond of this vegetable though our parents would tell us of its health benefits. And these days it has come into prominence because of its enormous impact on the treatment of high blood pressure and heart disease.

INGREDIENTS

250 grams bottle gourd (lauki), peeled, blanched and halved horizontally

3 tablespoons oil

1 tablespoon chopped fresh coriander

Stuffing

½ cup grated cottage cheese

1 teaspoon green chilli-ginger paste

2 tablespoons chopped fresh coriander

1 teaspoon dried mango powder

½ teaspoon coriander powder

½ teaspoon red chilli powder

¼ cup chopped mixed dried fruits

Salt to taste

Gravy

1 inch cinnamon

3 cloves

2 cups puréed tomatoes

2 teaspoons green chilli-ginger paste

1 teaspoon coriander powder

2 teaspoons red chilli powder

Salt to taste

½ teaspoon Garam Masala Powder (page 99)

1 teaspoon sugar

METHOD

1. Scoop out the pulp from the bottle gourd and discard it.
2. Heat one tablespoon oil in a non-stick pan. Cook the bottle gourd till light brown specks form on both sides and the gourd is cooked. Drain on absorbent paper and set aside.
3. To make the stuffing, mix together the cottage cheese, green chilli-ginger paste, chopped coriander, dried mango powder, coriander powder, chilli powder, mixed dried fruits and salt. Mix well.
4. Stuff the mixture into the cavity of the bottle gourd and pack it in firmly. Slice into two inch pieces.
5. Heat the remaining oil in the same pan and add the cinnamon and cloves. As they begin to change colour, add the tomato puree and sauté till the oil separates. Add the green chilli-ginger paste, coriander powder, chilli powder, salt, garam masala powder, sugar and mix well. Add one-fourth cup of water and let it simmer for a minute. Pour over the stuffed gourd while still hot.
7. Garnish with one tablespoon chopped coriander and serve hot.

{Kasuri Methi Paneer}

{Rajasthani Bharwan Lauki}

{Methi Mangodi}

{Turai Sabzi}

Methi Mangodi

INGREDIENTS

Mangodis are moong dal dumplings that can be sun-dried and stored to be used as and whenever you want to savour its taste. Here it combines well with fresh fenugreek leaves to make a dish that can be enjoyed with paranthe or rotis. You can also pack them in your tiffin. In that case make sure to pack more for your colleagues will want to taste it too.

2 cups chopped fresh fenugreek (methi), blanched

1 cup green gram dumplings (Mangodi) (page 99)

2 tablespoons oil + for deep-frying

1 tablespoon cumin seeds

½ teaspoon asafoetida

4 dried red chillies

1 tablespoon green chilli-ginger paste

2 medium tomatoes, chopped

Salt to taste

1 teaspoon Kashmiri red chilli powder

1 teaspoon turmeric powder

2 teaspoons coriander powder

1 teaspoon cumin powder

½ cup yogurt

1 tablespoon chopped fresh coriander

METHOD

1. Heat sufficient oil in a kadai and deep-fry the green gram dumplings till light golden. Drain and soak in two cups water for fifteen minutes.

2. Heat two tablespoons oil in a non-stick kadai and add the cumin seeds. When they begin to change colour, add the asafoetida, red chillies and sauté for one minute.

3. Add the green chilli-ginger paste and sauté for one minute.

4. Add the tomatoes and cook till the tomatoes turn pulpy. Add the fresh fenugreek and salt and cook for two to three minutes.

5. Add the chilli powder, turmeric powder, coriander powder, cumin powder and mix well. Add the green gram dumplings and mix. Cook for two to three minutes.

6. Add the yogurt and one cup water and let the gravy come to a boil.

7. Serve hot garnished with the chopped coriander.

Chef's Note: Mangodi, a Rajasthani speciality are dried green gram dumplings.

Turai Sabzi

Turai or ridge gourds are tropical vines. They are harvested before maturity and used to cook various dishes like chutney, or added to dal or made into a curry. In Maharashtra they are often prepared with either crushed dried peanuts or with beans. Here we have used chana dal which makes the dish wholesome.

INGREDIENTS

250 grams ridge gourd (turai), chopped

2 tablespoons oil

1 teaspoon cumin seeds

1 medium tomato, chopped

5 tablespoons split Bengal gram, soaked and drained

2 green chillies, broken

¼ teaspoon turmeric powder

½ teaspoon red chilli powder

Salt to taste

¼ teaspoon Garam Masala Powder (page 99)

1 tablespoon chopped fresh coriander

METHOD

1. Heat the oil in a non-stick pan and add the cumin seeds and sauté for one minute.
2. Add the tomato and mix well. Sauté till the oil separates.
3. Add the Bengal gram and mix well. Sauté for three to four minutes.
4. Add the green chillies, turmeric powder, chilli powder, salt, ridge gourd and one cup of water. Mix well, cover and bring it to a boil. Cook till both the gram and gourd are cooked. Add the garam masala powder and mix well.
5. Serve hot garnished with chopped coriander.

   (Image on page 54)

Makai Parantha

These are makai paranthe with a difference for here instead of using makai ka atta I have used makai ke daane. And I simply love the crunch the crushed corn adds to these paranthe. They really do make a great breakfast item served with a pickle of your choice. I like them even more with aam ka achaar.

INGREDIENTS

2 cups corn kernels, boiled and crushed

3 cups whole-wheat flour + for dusting

Salt to taste

½ cup yogurt

1 tablespoon oil + for shallow-frying

2 green chillies, finely chopped

1½ teaspoons red chilli powder

2 teaspoons Chaat Masala (page 99)

2 teaspoons roasted cumin powder

2 teaspoons dried mint powder

4 tablespoons chopped fresh coriander

METHOD

1. Mix the flour and salt in a bowl. Add the yogurt, one tablespoon oil and knead into a dough using water as needed. Cover with a damp cloth and rest for fifteen minutes.

2. Mix the corn, green chillies, chilli powder, chaat masala, cumin powder, dried mint powder, chopped coriander and salt.

3. Divide both the dough and filling into eight equal portions each.

4. Roll out each dough portion into a small puri. Place a portion of the filling in the center, gather the edges, pinch them together and roll into a ball. Allow the balls to rest for about fifteen minutes.

5. Lightly press each stuffed ball, dust with a little flour and roll out into one-eighth-inch thick paranthe. Shake off the excess flour.

6. Heat a non-stick tawa. Place a parantha on the tawa and roast on high heat for half a minute on both the sides. Lower the heat, drizzle a little oil and shallow-fry till the underside is golden. Flip over and drizzle some more oil and shallow-fry till the other side is golden too. Serve hot with pickle.

(Image on page 64)

Jalpari Biryani

Did the name mislead you into thinking that this is a fish biryani? Well here jalpari is lotus stems. Cooked with all the spices and condiments that go into making a biryani loaded with flavour, a plateful really fills me with joy of eating good food. Try it yourself.

INGREDIENTS

1½ cups Basmati rice, soaked for 2 hours and drained
125 grams lotus stems   5 tablespoons ghee
8-10 cashew nuts   1 tablespoon raisins   1 cup yogurt
1 teaspoon red chilli powder   1½ teaspoons garam masala powder (see page 123)
1½ teaspoons coriander powder   ½ teaspoon turmeric powder
1 teaspoon green cardamom powder   ½ cup boiled green peas
1 teaspoon screw pine water   1 teaspoon rose water   Salt to taste
2 inches ginger, cut into thin strips   2 tablespoons chopped fresh mint
2 green chillies, chopped   4 green cardamoms   1 inch cinnamon
1 black cardamom   A pinch of saffron, soaked in 2 tablespoons of milk
Whole-wheat flour dough for sealing

Masala Paste
⅓ cup fresh mint   4 tablespoons chopped fresh coriander   1-2 green chillies

METHOD

1. Soak the rice for two hours. Drain.
2. Peel the lotus stem and cut into strips. Soak in water.
3. To make the paste, grind the fresh mint and coriander with green chillies till smooth.
4. Heat the ghee in a large non-stick pan. Add the lotus stem strips and sauté for four minutes. Add the cashew nuts, raisins and sauté for three minutes. Add the ground paste, mix well and sauté for three minutes.
5. Place the yogurt in a bowl, add the chilli powder, garam masala powder, coriander powder, turmeric powder and cardamom powder and mix well.
6. Add the yogurt mixture, mix well and cook for five minutes. Add the green peas and mix well. Add half a teaspoon of screw pine water, half a teaspoon of rose water, salt, ginger, chopped mint and green chillies and mix well.
7. Boil four cups of water in a deep non-stick pan with green cardamoms, cinnamon, black cardamom, salt, remaining screw pine water and rose water. Add the rice and cook till half done. Strain in a colander.
8. Layer the rice over the lotus stem masala. Sprinkle the saffron-flavoured milk. Cover the pan and seal the edges with the dough and cook on dum on medium heat for five to ten minutes. Remove the seal and serve hot.

(Image on page 64)

Palak Methi Thepla

Methi thepla is a popular Gujarati snack. But it is not necessary that they be made in the same way each time. Deviate slightly and add spinach and see the difference. For spinach not only lends its emerald green colour, but also makes the theple more nutrition-dense.

INGREDIENTS

¼ cup shredded fresh spinach (palak)

¼ cup chopped fresh fenugreek (methi)

1 cup whole-wheat flour

¼ cup gram flour

¼ teaspoon turmeric powder

1 teaspoon red chilli powder

1 teaspoon ginger-green chilli paste

Salt to taste

4 tablespoons oil + for shallow-frying

6 tablespoons yogurt

METHOD

1. Place the flour, gram flour, spinach, fresh fenugreek, turmeric powder, chilli powder, ginger-green chilli paste, salt and four tablespoons of oil in a deep bowl and mix well.
2. Add the yogurt and knead into a semi-soft dough. Cover with a damp cloth and set aside for fifteen minutes.
3. Divide the dough into twelve equal portions and shape into balls. Roll out each ball into six-inch diameter theplas.
4. Heat a non-stick tawa. Place a thepla on it and cook turning sides and applying oil on each side, till both the sides are evenly golden.
5. Serve hot or cold.

   (Image on page 65)

Rajasthani Pulao With Chana Dal

All the way from the royal kitchens of Rajasthan is this flavourful pulao. Most Rajasthanis are Jains who refrain from consuming onions and garlic and all other root vegetables. Yet their food is ever so tasty and this pulao is just one proof of that.

INGREDIENTS

1 ½ cups rice, soaked for 2 hours

¼ cup split Bengal gram, (chana dal) soaked overnight and drained

4 tablespoons ghee

1 inch cinnamon

2 cloves

2 green cardamoms

1 black cardamom

1 bay leaf

1 teaspoon cumin seeds

5-6 black peppercorns

3 teaspoons red chilli powder

½ teaspoon turmeric powder

1 ½ teaspoons coriander powder

Salt to taste

1 ½ tablespoons dried mint leaves

METHOD

1. Heat the ghee in a deep non-stick pan; add the cinnamon, cloves, both cardamoms, bay leaf, cumin seeds, peppercorns and sauté for one minute.

2. Add the chilli powder, turmeric powder, coriander powder and salt. Cook for a few seconds and add the gram.

3. Once the ghee separates from the masalas, add three cups of water and bring it to a boil. Add the dried mint.

4. Add the rice and cook till done. Serve hot.

(Image on page 66)

Adai

Adai is a high protein dish, very similar to dosa, though it is a little heavier. You can even call it a distant cousin of North Indian chilla. It is gluten free since it is made by blending lentils with rice. It is also a rich source of dietary fiber and above all it is also ever so delicious and wholesome. Ideal dish to make for a Sunday brunch.

INGREDIENTS

1 cup parboiled rice, soaked

¼ cup split skinless black gram, soaked

¼ cup split skinless green gram, soaked

¼ cup split Bengal gram, soaked

¼ cup split pigeon pea, soaked

Salt to taste

¼ teaspoon turmeric powder

¼ teaspoon asafoetida

1 tablespoon oil + for cooking

½ teaspoon mustard seeds

2 dried red chillies, seeded and chopped

7-8 curry leaves, chopped

2 green chillies, chopped

½ inch ginger, chopped

METHOD

1. Soak the rice and gram overnight or for at least eight hours. Drain and grind together with a little water. Add the salt, turmeric powder and asafoetida and grind till smooth. Transfer into a bowl.

2. Heat one tablespoon of oil in a small non-stick pan; add the mustard seeds. When the mustard seeds splutter add the red chillies and curry leaves and sauté for a few seconds. Add the seasoning to the batter and mix well. Add the green chillies and ginger and mix well.

3. Heat a non-stick tawa and grease it lightly. Spread a ladleful of batter to a medium-sized round adai and cook till the underside is golden.

4. Drizzle a little oil over it, turn it over and cook till both sides are evenly golden and crisp. Serve hot.

(Image on page 63)

Spinach And Carrot Rice

My mother-in-law is a great cook and very good at inventing new concoctions. This is her recipe which she used to cook often when Alyona and her sisters were school-going. They, like most other children, used to make a lot of fuss to eat vegetables so their mother would ensure that they ate them by cooking them in different ways

INGREDIENTS

2 cups fresh spinach, shredded

2 medium carrots, grated

1 ½ cups Basmati rice, soaked and drained

2 tablespoons ghee

½ teaspoons fennel seeds

2 black cardamoms

1 inch cinnamon

2 cloves

Salt to taste

¼ teaspoon red chilli powder

2 teaspoons lemon juice

METHOD

1. Heat the ghee in a non-stick pan. Add the fennel seeds, black cardamoms, cinnamon and cloves and sauté till fennel seeds begin to change colour.
2. Add the spinach and grated carrots and sauté for one minute.
3. Add the rice and sauté for one minute. Add the salt and chilli powder and mix well.
4. Add three cups of water and mix well. Cook till it comes to a boil, then lower the heat and cook covered for twelve to fifteen minutes or until the rice is done. Add lemon juice and mix well.
5. Serve hot with any raita.

{Spinach and Carrot Rice}

{Adai}

{Makai Parantha}

{Jalpari Biryani}

{Matar Wadiwale Chawal}

{Palak Methi Thepla}

{Rajasthani Pulao with Chana Dal}

{Kacche Papite
ke Paranthe}

Kachche Papite Ke Paranthe

The high content of beneficial enzymes and antioxidants make papaya an excellent remedy for many health disorders and diseases. It is known to strengthen our immune and digestive systems and also protect against free radicals. Unripe papaya paste is also used as a tenderiser while preparing mutton dishes. Serve them immediately to get the best flavour.

INGREDIENTS

1 small unripe papaya (kachcha papita), peeled and grated

1½ cups whole-wheat flour + for dusting ▲ Salt to taste ▲ 2 tablespoons oil

¼ teaspoon turmeric powder ▲ 2-3 green chillies, finely chopped

¼ cup chopped fresh coriander ▲ ½ teaspoon red chilli powder

2 teaspoons dried mango powder ▲ Ghee for shallow-frying

METHOD

1. Mix together the whole-wheat flour, salt and two tablespoons of oil in a bowl. Add sufficient water and knead into soft dough. Cover with damp cloth and rest for fifteen minutes.
2. Place the grated papaya in a bowl; add salt and set aside for ten to fifteen minutes.
3. Squeeze out excess water from the papaya and transfer into another bowl. Add the turmeric powder, green chillies, chopped coriander, chilli powder and dried mango powder and mix. Check the seasonings. Divide into eight equal portions.
4. Divide the dough into sixteen equal portions and shape into balls.
5. For each parantha, roll out one dough ball into a one-eighth-inch thick puri and place a portion of stuffing in the centre. Roll another dough ball similarly and place on top of first puri with the stuffing and press the edges to seal. Dust some flour and roll out into a thick parantha.
6. Heat a non-stick tawa. Place the parantha on it and roast for one minute. Turn over and drizzle some ghee around it. Turn over again and drizzle some more ghee all around and shallow-fry, turning sides, till evenly golden brown on both the sides.
7. Serve hot with your choice of chutney or tomato ketchup or yogurt.

Matar Wadiwale Chawal

Every time we got Amritsari urad dal wadis, the obvious dish we cooked was wadiyan aloo. So once I thought why not make something different. These wadis are spicy and have a wonderful smoky flavour. So here it is something different, cooked with rice and green peas.

INGREDIENTS

½ cup shelled green peas (matar)

4 Amritsari urad dal wadi, crushed coarsely

1½ cups rice, soaked and drained

2 tablespoons oil

½ teaspoon cumin seeds

1 green chilli, slit

1 teaspoon turmeric powder

1 teaspoon red chilli powder

½ cup yogurt

Salt to taste

3 tablespoons chopped fresh coriander

METHOD

1. Heat the oil in a deep non-stick pan and add the cumin seeds. When they begin to change colour, add the green chilli, crushed wadi and green peas and sauté till fragrant.

2. Add the turmeric powder and chilli powder and sauté for half a minute. Add the yogurt and sauté till the oil separates.

3. Add the rice, salt and four cups water and mix well. When the mixture comes to a boil, cover and cook on medium heat till the rice is done.

4. Garnish with the chopped coriander and serve hot.

(Image on page 65)

Aloo aur Khumb Biryani

Mushrooms have always been my all time favourite vegetable...I mean fungii. The best thing about mushrooms are that they take on any flavour and yet retain their very own special taste. In this biryani, the special effect is that of mace powder which makes it ever so flavourful. Simply yummy....

INGREDIENTS

2 medium potatoes (aloo), diced   200 grams fresh button mushrooms (khumb), quartered   1½ cups Basmati rice, soaked and drained   Salt to taste   1 teaspoon mace powder   1 inch cinnamon   2-3 green cardamoms   5 tablespoons oil   1 medium tomato, chopped   1 teaspoon red chilli powder   ½ teaspoon turmeric powder   ½ cup yogurt   ½ teaspoon Garam Masala Powder (page 99)   4 tablespoons chopped fresh coriander   1 teaspoon screw pine water   1 teaspoon rose water   3 tablespoons ghee   1 teaspoon saffron soaked in 2 teaspoons of milk   1 teaspoon green cardamom powder

METHOD

1. Boil six to eight cups water with salt, half teaspoon mace powder, cinnamon and green cardamoms in a deep non-stick pan. Add the rice and cook till nearly done. Drain in a colander and set aside.
2. Heat the oil in a non-stick pan. Add the tomato and sauté till pulpy. Add the chilli powder and turmeric powder. Mix well and sauté till the oil separates.
3. Reduce the heat and add the yogurt and continue sautéing, stirring continuously. Cook till the gravy turns thick. Add the potatoes and cook for five minutes. Add the salt, garam masala powder and the chopped coriander. Add the mushrooms and cook till they are soft.
4. Add the screw pine water and rose water. Mix well.
5. To assemble the biryani, spread half the potato-mushroom mixture in a non-stick pan. Top it with half the rice and drizzle half the ghee and half the saffron-flavoured milk. Repeat these layers once.
6. Sprinkle remaining mace powder and cardamom powder. Cover the pan with a lid and cook on dum for ten minutes. Serve hot.

Mango Rice

This is a savoury preparation where I have combined rice with unripe mango, peanuts and coconut. During the mango season, this dish is prepared quite often at our home. In fact I always request Alyona to cook a little extra so that she can pack it in the tiffin too. And it tastes quite good when cold too.

INGREDIENTS

2 medium unripe green mangoes, peeled and grated

3 cups cooked rice

1 ½ tablespoons roasted peanuts

4 tablespoons freshly grated coconut

½ teaspoon turmeric powder

1 tablespoon oil

¼ teaspoon mustard seeds

¼ teaspoon cumin seeds

A large pinch of asafoetida

20 curry leaves

2 dried red chillies

Salt to taste

1 ½ tablespoons ghee

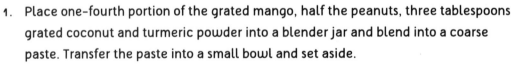

METHOD

1. Place one-fourth portion of the grated mango, half the peanuts, three tablespoons grated coconut and turmeric powder into a blender jar and blend into a coarse paste. Transfer the paste into a small bowl and set aside.

2. Heat the oil in a large non-stick frying pan. Add the mustard seeds. When the seeds begin to splutter add the cumin seeds, asafoetida, curry leaves and red chillies and sauté for one minute.

3. Add the prepared paste and remaining peanuts and sauté for one minute.

4. Add the cooked rice and mix well.

5. Add the remaining grated mango, salt and toss well till heated through.

6. Transfer the rice into a serving dish.

7. Drizzle the ghee all over the rice and garnish with the remaining grated coconut. Serve hot.

Bhature

If you are making chole, can bhature be far behind? Made of fermented refined flour dough, bhature puff up beautifully. But yes they do absorb a lot of oil. But you can have them once in a while, as long as you make up for those extra calories consumed by exercising a little more.

INGREDIENTS

2½ cups refined flour

½ teaspoon baking powder

A pinch of baking soda (soda bicarbonate)

Salt to taste

½ cup yogurt

2 teaspoons sugar

2 tablespoons oil + for deep-frying

METHOD

1. Sift the flour, baking powder, baking soda and salt together into a deep bowl.
2. Mix the yogurt with sugar. Add this to the flour and add about a cup of water and mix gradually to make a soft dough. Knead lightly.
3. Incorporate two tablespoons of oil into the dough and cover it with a damp cloth. Set it aside for an hour.
4. Divide the dough into sixteen equal portions and roll them into balls. Cover and set aside for ten more minutes.
5. Grease your palms with a little oil and flatten the balls. Roll out each into a five-inch diameter round.
6. Heat sufficient oil in a kadai and deep-fry the bhature, one at a time, on high heat, till light brown on both sides.
7. Drain on absorbent paper. Serve hot with Chole (page 49).

Chef's Tip: You can make oval-shaped bhature by pulling the rounds from opposite sides.

Masala Puri

These are ideal tea time treats. My mother makes namak ajwain ke paranthe very often. The same dough can be made into puris. When we were trying out these puris in our trial kitchen the puris had been devoured within minutes. Need I say any more about them?

INGREDIENTS

2 cups whole-wheat flour

1 tablespoon coriander powder

1 teaspoon turmeric powder

2 tablespoons red chilli powder

2 tablespoons chopped dried oregano

Salt to taste

2 tablespoons yogurt

Oil for deep-frying

METHOD

1. Place the flour in a deep bowl. Add the coriander powder, turmeric powder, chilli powder, oregano, salt and yogurt and mix well. Knead into a soft dough using water as required.

2. Cover and rest for ten minutes.

3. Divide into twenty small portions and roll into balls. Roll out into small puris.

4. Heat sufficient oil in a kadai and deep-fry the puri till golden brown on both the sides. Drain on absorbent paper.

5. Serve hot with yogurt or chutney.

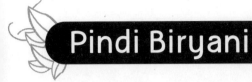

Pindi Biryani

The transition from pindi chole to pindi biryani was not surprising. Normally pindi chole are eaten with bhature or puris. But cooked this way with rice, it is definitely healthier. My earnest suggestion to all the foodies is make this biryani immediately and you will never regret the effort.

INGREDIENTS

1 cup Basmati rice

1 cup chickpeas

2 tablespoons tea leaves

Salt to taste

5-6 green cardamoms

2-3 bay leaves

2-3 cloves

1½ cups yogurt

1 teaspoon ginger paste

1 inch ginger, cut into thin strips

½ cup fresh mint, hand torn

1 teaspoon green chilli paste

1 teaspoon red chilli powder

1 teaspoon turmeric powder

1 teaspoon Garam Masala Powder
(page 99)

A few strands of saffron, dissolved in 2 tablespoons of water

A few drops of screw pine water

2 tablespoons chopped fresh coriander

METHOD

1. Soak the chickpeas overnight in four cups of water. Drain and pressure-cook in four cups of water with tea leaves tied in a piece of muslin and salt till tender. Remove the muslin bag and drain the chickpeas.

2. Soak the rice in three cups of water for about half an hour. Drain. Boil four cups of water in a deep non-stick pan with salt and green cardamoms, bay leaves and cloves. Add the rice and cook till half done. Drain excess water.

3. Marinate the boiled chickpeas in the yogurt, ginger paste, ginger strips, half the fresh mint, green chilli paste, chilli powder, turmeric powder and garam masala powder for fifteen minutes.

4. Place the marinated chickpeas in a deep non-stick pan. Spread cooked rice over evenly. Sprinkle saffron water, screw pine water and half the chopped coriander.

5. Cover the pan tightly and cook on low heat for fifteen minutes or till rice is cooked.

6. Garnish with the remaining fresh coriander and mint. Serve hot

Amla and Green Chilli Pickle

Amla or Indian gooseberry is very rich in vitamin C and also has powerful antioxidants which protect us from harmful free radicals that can cause serious diseases including cancer. I like experimenting with different ingredients and I have made quite a few different things with amla. But this pickle is something I had at a friend's place and simply fell in love with it. Here it is for you.

INGREDIENTS

500 grams Indian gooseberries (amla), cut into cubes

1 cup green chillies, slit

5 tablespoons mustard oil

½ teaspoon mustard seeds

¼ teaspoon asafoetida

½ teaspoon fenugreek seeds

4 teaspoons red chilli powder

½ inch ginger, grated

Salt to taste

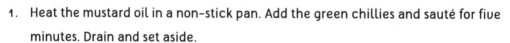

METHOD

1. Heat the mustard oil in a non-stick pan. Add the green chillies and sauté for five minutes. Drain and set aside.

2. To the oil remaining in the pan, add the mustard seeds, asafoetida, fenugreek seeds and sauté for a minute.

3. Add the gooseberries and sauté for five minutes. Add the chilli powder, grated ginger and sauté for a minute. Add half cup of water and cook till the gooseberries become soft.

4. Add the fried green chillies and salt and mix well.

5. Store in an air-tight container.

{Ghiya Raita}

{Amla and Green Chilli Pickle}

{Arhar Dal with Palak}

{Tomato Chutney with Dates}

Arhar Dal with Palak

You just cannot have enough of spinach, a wonderful green-leafy vegetable which is full of nutritional goodness such as antioxidants and anti-cancer constituents. Its tender, crispy, dark-green leaves are favoured by most chefs around the world for it is so very easy to cook up wonderful things with it. Do ensure that they are not overcooked so that their lovely green colour is retained.

INGREDIENTS

1 cup split pigeon peas (arhar dal/toovar dal)

30-40 fresh spinach leaves (palak), roughly shredded

Salt to taste

1 teaspoon turmeric powder

2 tablespoons oil

A pinch of asafoetida

1 teaspoon cumin seeds

2 green chillies, chopped

1 inch ginger, chopped

1 teaspoon lemon juice

METHOD

1. Cook the split pigeon peas with salt, turmeric powder and five cups of water in a pressure cooker, till the pressure is released twice (two whistles).
2. Heat the oil in a non-stick kadai. Add the asafoetida and cumin seeds. When the cumin seeds begin to change colour, add the green chillies, ginger and sauté for half a minute.
3. Add the dal and bring to a boil. Stir in the spinach and lemon juice.
4. Simmer for two minutes and serve hot.

Tomato Chutney With Dates

Tomato chutney can be made variously. In fact practically in each state of India tomato chutney is made and all of them have a distinct taste, texture and flavour. This chutney is made in South Indian style. Try it out, it can be savoured with dosa or idli. I like it as a sandwich spread.

INGREDIENTS

6 medium tomatoes, cut into cubes

12-14 seedless dates, chopped

1 teaspoon oil

Salt to taste

1 teaspoon chopped fresh coriander

Masala

4 teaspoons oil

½ teaspoon asafoetida

4 teaspoons skinless split black gram

2 teaspoons mustard seeds

6-7 dried red chillies, broken

2 green chillies, chopped roughly

METHOD

1. To make the masala, heat the oil in a non-stick pan. Add the asafoetida, black gram and mustard seeds. When the mustard seeds start to splutter, add the red chillies and sauté for a few seconds.
2. Add the green chillies and sauté for a few seconds. Take the pan off the heat and when the contents have cooled, transfer into a blender jar. Set aside.
3. Heat one teaspoon oil in the same pan and add the tomatoes and chopped dates. Sauté till soft. Take the pan off the heat and transfer the tomatoes and dates mixture into a bowl and cool.
4. Add two tablespoons water to the blender jar and grind the masala mixture to a coarse paste. Add the tomatoes-dates mixture and salt and grind again. Transfer into a bowl. Add the chopped coriander and mix. Serve.

(Image on page 76)

Ghiya Raita

Ideal for the weight-watchers, ghiya or bottle gourd has numerous health benefits. Its juice is used not only to treat jaundice but also acidity, indigestion and ulcers. It is also rich in essential minerals, protein and fibre making it a vegetable that should be included in your menu often.

INGREDIENTS

250 grams bottle gourd (ghiya/lauki/doodhi)

Salt to taste

3 cups yogurt, chilled

½ teaspoon red chilli powder

1 teaspoon cumin seeds

METHOD

1. Peel and grate the bottle gourd. Place in a small non-stick pan with one cup of water and a little salt and cook for five minutes. Drain out water and let the bottle gourd cool. Squeeze out the excess water.
2. Whisk the chilled yogurt and add the salt and chilli powder. Mix well and add the bottle gourd and mix again.
3. Dry-roast cumin seeds and pound to a coarse powder. Sprinkle on the raita and serve.

(Image on page 75)

Daalia Chutney

Made with roasted chana dal, this chutney has a unique taste that goes excellently with the famous Maharashtrian snack – thalipeeth. This is a favoured breakfast item at our place. And we have it at least once a week.

INGREDIENTS

¾ cup roasted split Bengal gram (daalia)

1 green chilli, chopped

Salt to taste

½ teaspoon cumin seeds

1 cup yogurt

1 tablespoon oil

¼ teaspoon mustard seeds

1 dried red chilli, broken

5-6 curry leaves

¼ teaspoon turmeric powder

METHOD

1. Grind together roasted gram, green chilli, salt and cumin seeds in a blender. Transfer the mixture into a bowl. Add the yogurt and mix well.

2. Heat the oil in a non-stick pan. Add the mustard seeds, red chilli, curry leaves and turmeric powder and sauté till the seeds splutter. Add this seasoning to the chutney and mix well. Serve.

Pomegranate Raita

This raita is as tasty as it looks good. Choose a pomegranate that has ruby red kernels which will lend its brightness to the yogurt which, with the emerald green of the mint leaves, makes this raita look like a bowlful of gems. Besides these red gems contain nutrients that aid in lowering cholesterol and preventing muscle cramps.

INGREDIENTS

½ cup pomegranate kernels

1 ½ cups yogurt, whisked

10-12 fresh mint

1 teaspoon roasted cumin powder

½ teaspoon powdered sugar

Black salt to taste

Salt to taste

METHOD

1. Reserve four to five fresh mint for garnishing and finely chop the rest.
2. Combine the pomegranate kernels, yogurt, chopped mint, roasted cumin powder, sugar, black salt and salt in a large bowl. Chill in the refrigerator for about thirty minutes.
3. Serve garnished with the reserved fresh mint.

Aam Pickle

The ubiquitous mango pickle is indeed a favourite of everyone. I distinctly recollect the pickle-making session at home in Delhi when my mother would cut mounds of unripe mango, salt them, add masala and plenty of mustard oil and then sun-dry in huge porcelain jars which we call martban. After sun-drying them for a good three to four days the pickle should be allowed to mature for around fifteen days before serving.

INGREDIENTS

1 kilogram whole unripe green mangoes (aam)

750 ml filtered mustard oil

250 grams salt

50 grams turmeric powder

50 grams red chilli powder

100 grams crushed fennel seeds

50 grams crushed fenugreek seeds

200 grams chickpeas

METHOD

1. Wash and wipe the mangoes completely dry. Cut them into half, remove the seed letting the hard endocarp remain. Further cut them into one-inch cubes.
2. Heat the mustard oil in a non-stick pan till it starts to smoke. Set aside to cool.
3. Place the mango cubes, salt, turmeric powder, chilli powder, fennel seeds, fenugreek seeds and chickpeas in a large sterilised porcelain jar and mix. Add half the oil and mix.
4. Cover the jar with piece of muslin, tied with a string round the rim and keep in the sun for three to four days. Remember to mix the contents at least once a day.
5. Add the remaining oil and let the pickle mature for fifteen days.
6. It lasts for one year.

Chef's Tip: A layer of oil on the top serves as a preservative.

Chickpea Salad

Chole is not the only thing that we can cook up with chickpeas or kabuli chane. In our refrigerator you will always find a lot of boiled kabuli chane so that we churn up some wonderful things with them in a jiffy. Wholesome and piquant, it is a salad but it can be had as an anytime snack.

INGREDIENTS

1 ½ cups chickpeas, soaked overnight and boiled till soft

2 small potatoes, boiled, peeled and cut into small cubes

2 small tomatoes, chopped

2 teaspoons chopped fresh coriander

1 green chilli, chopped

2-3 teaspoons lemon juice

¼ teaspoon black salt

Salt to taste

2 teaspoons Chaat Masala (page 99)

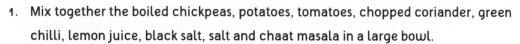

METHOD

1. Mix together the boiled chickpeas, potatoes, tomatoes, chopped coriander, green chilli, lemon juice, black salt, salt and chaat masala in a large bowl.

2. Toss all the ingredients well to mix. Serve immediately.

    (Image on page 85)

Panchratni Dal

As the name suggests it is a preparation made with the mixture of five different types of dal. This flavourful dal from Rajasthan is also known as panchmel dal. It makes a nutritious meal with hot rice or chapati. You can also serve it with the famous Rajasthani baati and dollops of ghee.
Absolute manna.

INGREDIENTS

2 tablespoons whole red lentils
2 tablespoons whole black gram
2 tablespoons whole green gram
2 tablespoons split Bengal gram
2 tablespoons split pigeon peas
2 teaspoons oil
2 green cardamoms, crushed
1 inch cinnamon
½ teaspoon caraway seeds

1 small tomato, chopped
1 teaspoon coriander powder
$1/3$ teaspoon roasted cumin powder
¼ teaspoon turmeric powder
1 teaspoon fennel powder
1 ½ teaspoons red chilli powder
$1/3$ cup skimmed milk yogurt, whisked
Salt to taste
½ tablespoon fresh cream

METHOD

1. Soak all the lentils in two cups of water for an hour and a half. Drain and set aside.
2. Place all the lentils with three cups water in a pressure cooker. Cover with the lid and cook over medium heat till the pressure is released four times (four whistles). Open the lid when the pressure has reduced completely.
3. Heat the oil in a deep non-stick pan and add the cardamoms, cinnamon and caraway seeds and sauté till fragrant.
4. Add the tomato, coriander powder, cumin powder, turmeric powder, fennel powder and chilli powder and sauté for two to three minutes.
5. Add the yogurt and cook for two minutes more.
6. Add the cooked lentils, two-third cup of water and salt and allow the mixture to come to a boil. Serve hot, garnished with the cream.

{Panchratni Dal}

{Chickpea Salad}

{Sindhi Kadhi}

{Fruit and Nut Salad}

Sindhi Kadhi

The different vegetables used in Sindhi kadhi merge together beautifully to give the kadhi a wonderful taste, colour and texture. You will find this in practically every Sindhi home on Sundays when the entire family sits together and enjoys the kadhi with hot steamed rice and may be alu tuk and sweet boondi.

INGREDIENTS

3 medium potatoes

5 tablespoons oil

1 teaspoon cumin seeds

1 teaspoon fenugreek seeds

¾ cup gram flour

10–12 curry leaves

2 green chillies, chopped

1 inch ginger, grated

Salt to taste

½ teaspoon turmeric powder

¼ cup shelled green peas

2 medium drumsticks, cut into 2-inch pieces

75 grams cluster beans, trimmed

100 grams ladies' fingers, trimmed

2 large tomatoes, finely chopped

2½ tablespoons Tamarind Pulp (page 100)

1½ teaspoons red chilli powder

3 tablespoons chopped fresh coriander

METHOD

1. Peel and cut each potato into half vertically and then cut into half horizontally.
2. Heat four tablespoons oil in a deep non-stick pan. Add the cumin seeds and fenugreek seeds and sauté for a few seconds.
3. Lower the heat, add the gram flour and sauté for six to eight minutes or till the flour is brown and fragrant.
4. Add four cups water and bring it to a boil. Add the curry leaves, green chillies and ginger and stir. Add the salt and turmeric powder and stir. Add the green peas, drumsticks and cluster beans. Cover the pan and simmer for ten minutes. Add the potatoes and cook for twenty minutes.
5. Heat the remaining oil in a small non-stick pan and add the ladies' fingers. Sauté for three to four minutes and add to the rest of the vegetables.
6. Add the tomatoes, tamarind pulp and chilli powder to the pan and stir. Cover the pan and cook for ten minutes.
7. Garnish with the chopped coriander and serve hot with steamed rice.

Fruit And Nut Salad

What could be more nutritious than the combination of fresh fruit and nuts? You can change the fruit and also the nuts to your taste. The mayonnaise and green chutney add a lovely spicy smoothness and also make the salad wholesome.

INGREDIENTS

2 tinned peaches, halved and cut into ½-inch pieces

6-7 seedless dates, halved

¼ cup cashew nuts, roasted

¼ cup Eggless Mayonnaise (page 99)

2 teaspoons green chutney

¼ bunch fresh lettuce, shredded

1 teaspoon tomato ketchup

Salt to taste

1 medium tomato, sliced

METHOD

1. Mix the mayonnaise and green chutney in a large bowl. Add the shredded lettuce, mix and arrange at the bottom of deep glass bowl.
2. Place the dates, tomato ketchup, peaches, cashew nuts and salt in another bowl and toss lightly.
3. Arrange on top of the lettuce.
4. Garnish with the tomato slices and serve immediately.
   (Image on page 86)

Ghughni

I've got you this dish all the way from Bengal. Yes it is a very popular street food there and I had tasted it for the first time on the streets of Kolkata, where it is served chaat-style. It also goes well with puris or luchis or even with paranthe.

INGREDIENTS

1 cup yellow dried peas

Salt to taste

3 tablespoons oil

2 tablespoons thinly sliced fresh coconut

½ teaspoon cumin seeds

2 bay leaves

1 teaspoon ginger paste

4-5 green chillies, chopped

2 medium tomatoes, puréed

1 tablespoon coriander powder

½ teaspoon cumin powder

½ teaspoon red chilli powder

¾ teaspoon turmeric powder

½ teaspoon Garam Masala Powder (page 99)

3 tablespoons tamarind pulp

2 tablespoons chopped fresh coriander

METHOD

1. Wash and soak the dried peas in three cups of water overnight in a large bowl.
2. Boil six cups of water in a deep non-stick pan. Add the peas and one teaspoon salt. When the mixture comes to a boil again, reduce heat to medium, cover the pan and cook till the peas are completely cooked and soft. Set aside.
3. Heat one tablespoon oil in another non-stick pan. Add the coconut pieces and sauté till golden brown. Drain and set aside.
4. Add the remaining oil to the same pan. Add the cumin seeds, bay leaves, ginger paste and green chillies and sauté for one minute.
5. Add the tomato purée and continue to sauté till the oil separates.
6. Add the coriander powder, cumin powder, chilli powder and turmeric powder and stir well. Add the cooked peas alongwith the cooking liquid and simmer for five minutes or till the gravy thickens.
7. Add the garam masala powder, stir well and put the ghughni into a serving bowl.
8. While serving, pour the ghughni into individual bowls, top it with the tamarind pulp, browned coconut slices and chopped coriander. Serve hot.

Dal Maharani

You may well ask why this dal is called as such. It is perhaps because cooked as it is with ghee, butter and cream it really is fit for a queen. But we ordinary mortals can enjoy it as well, can't we?

INGREDIENTS

½ cup whole black gram

2 tablespoons red kidney beans

Salt to taste

1 teaspoon red chilli powder

1 inch ginger, chopped

1 tablespoon pure ghee

2 tablespoons butter

1 teaspoon cumin seeds

1 medium tomato, chopped

1 teaspoon Garam Masala Powder (page 99)

¼ cup cream

METHOD

1. Soak the whole black gram and red kidney beans overnight in five cups of water. Drain.
2. Pressure-cook the soaked grams and beans in five cups of water with salt, chilli powder and ginger till the pressure is released eight times (eight whistles).
3. Heat the ghee and butter in a non-stick pan on medium heat and add the cumin seeds. When they begin to change colour, add the tomato and sauté till the tomato is pulpy and the oil separates.
4. Add the boiled gram, beans and one cup of water. Bring to a boil. Add the garam masala powder and cook on low heat for fifteen minutes. Stir in the cream and simmer for five minutes more.
5. Serve hot with naan or parantha.

Chef's Tip: This dish tastes just as good reheated the following day! But it also tastes delicious eaten cold with hot paranthe!

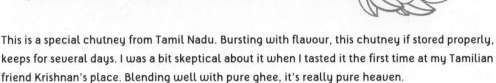

Kadipatta Chutney

This is a special chutney from Tamil Nadu. Bursting with flavour, this chutney if stored properly, keeps for several days. I was a bit skeptical about it when I tasted it the first time at my Tamilian friend Krishnan's place. Blending well with pure ghee, it's really pure heaven.

INGREDIENTS

2 cups curry leaves (kadipatta)

¼ cup roasted split Bengal gram

20-25 black peppercorns

Marble-sized tamarind ball

Salt to taste

METHOD

1. Roast the curry leaves, gram, peppercorns and tamarind one by one till dry and crisp. Mix well. Set aside to cool.
2. Transfer into a mixer jar and grind to a powder. Add salt and mix well.
3. Cool completely and store in an airtight container.
4. Tastes wonderful mixed with hot steamed rice and pure ghee.

Jigarthanda

Origins of Jigarthanda can be traced to the city of Madurai in Tamil Nadu. Apparently it was popularised by the Muslim settlers and you get the most authentic form in this city. In Hindi jigar means heart and thanda means cool, an apt name for a drink that is served during the hot summer months. I found it to be very similar to kulfi-falooda that we get in Mumbai.

INGREDIENTS

1 cup rabdi

1 cup kesari falooda

4 tablespoons sabza, soaked

4 thick round slices malai kulfi

4 tablespoons rose syrup

METHOD

1. Take four tall glasses. In each glass, place one tablespoon of sabza at the base. Over the sabza, place one-fourth cup of rabdi followed by one-fourth cup of kesari falooda.

2. Top with a slice of malai kulfi. Drizzle rose syrup and serve immediately.

Notes: 1) Falooda is vermicelli made of arrowroot.

2) Sabza is the Hindi word for basil seeds.

Chana Dal Kheer

This kheer is called madgane by the Saraswat Brahmins who make it as an offering to Lord Ganesh during Ganesh Chaturthi. But it is so very yummy that I for one wonder why it should be made only for the festival. I can enjoy it anytime and so would you once you have tasted it.

INGREDIENTS

½ cup split Bengal gram (chana dal)

½ cup cashew nuts, halved

1 cup grated jaggery

1 ½ cups freshly extracted thin coconut milk

2 tablespoons rice flour

1 cup freshly extracted thick coconut milk

½ teaspoon green cardamom powder

METHOD

1. Soak the Bengal gram in one and a half cups of water for an hour. Drain and cook along with cashew nuts in one cup of water till soft, taking care that the gram is not mashed.

2. Mix the jaggery in half a cup of water and stir till the jaggery dissolves. Strain into a deep non-stick pan to remove any impurities. Add the thin coconut milk and cook on low heat till it comes to a boil.

3. Mix the rice flour in half a cup of water and make a smooth paste. Add this paste to the simmering jaggery mixture and cook, stirring continuously to avoid any lumps from forming. Continue to cook on low heat till the rice flour is cooked. Add the cooked dal along with the cashew nuts and mix well.

4. Add the thick coconut milk and cardamom powder. Mix well and take off the heat when the mixture comes to a boil.

5. Serve with khotte (a kind of idli steamed in jackfruit leaf cones).

(Image on page 95)

Churma Laddoo

A traditional Rajasthani sweet, churma laddoo is made during festivals. It is quite nutritious too, as it is with whole-wheat flour and jaggery but that does not mean you just gorge on them. Remember there is plenty of ghee too. So enjoy them and then, you know what you have to. Yes indeed run a mile more to make up for the indulgence.

INGREDIENTS

2 cups coarse whole-wheat flour   4 tablespoons ghee + for deep-frying

¾ cup grated jaggery   ¼ cup (30 grams) powdered sugar

1 teaspoon green cardamom powder   1 teaspoon nutmeg powder

Poppy seeds, as required

METHOD

1. Place the flour in a bowl; add two tablespoons of hot ghee and gently rub it in with your fingertips. Add sufficient warm water and knead into a stiff dough. Divide the dough into four equal portions and shape them into small oval-shaped croquettes.
2. Heat sufficient ghee in a kadai and deep-fry the croquettes till golden brown. Drain on absorbent paper, break into smaller pieces and set aside to cool.
3. When completely cool, grind the pieces to a powder. Pass the powder through a sieve. Grind the residue remaining in the sieve to a fine powder and add to the sifted powder.
4. Heat two tablespoons of ghee in another non-stick pan. Add the jaggery and cook, stirring, till it melts. Remove from the heat and add the sifted powder and mix well. Add the powdered sugar and mix.
5. Add the cardamom powder and nutmeg powder, and mix well.
6. Divide the mixture into sixteen equal portions and shape each portion into a laddoo. Roll the laddoo in the poppy seeds.
7. Cool and store in an airtight container.

{Churma Laddoo}

{Chana Dal Kheer}

{Mishti Doi}

{Kesar Bhaat}

Kesar Bhaat

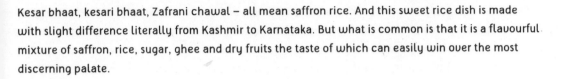

Kesar bhaat, kesari bhaat, Zafrani chawal – all mean saffron rice. And this sweet rice dish is made with slight difference literally from Kashmir to Karnataka. But what is common is that it is a flavourful mixture of saffron, rice, sugar, ghee and dry fruits the taste of which can easily win over the most discerning palate.

INGREDIENTS

A few threads of saffron

1 cup Basmati rice, soaked

1 tablespoon pure ghee

2 tablespoons raisins

7-8 cashew nuts, halved

½ cup sugar

½ teaspoon green cardamom powder

25 grams sugar crystals

METHOD

1. Dissolve the saffron in one tablespoon of warm water and set aside.

2. Heat the ghee in a non-stick pan; sauté the raisins and cashew nuts till lightly browned. Drain and set aside. In the same ghee add the rice and sauté for two to three minutes.

3. Add one and a half cups of boiling water along with saffron-flavoured water and let the rice cook.

4. When half done add the sugar and continue to cook till all the water has been absorbed and the rice is cooked.

5. Add the cardamom powder and mix gently.

6. Decorate with raisins, cashew nuts and sugar crystals. Serve hot.

Mishti Doi

Mishti Doi is perhaps the most popular of Bengali sweets and when translated it means sweet curd. No festival or special occasion for the Bengalis can be complete without bowls full of mishti doi. The curd is set in earthen pots which lend their very own special flavour. Usually caramalised sugar is used to sweeten the curd but during season notun gud or nolen gud is added which makes the doi absolutely heavenly.

INGREDIENTS

1 litre milk

2 teaspoons yogurt

1 cup sugar

METHOD

1. Boil the milk till it is reduced to half. Remove from heat and leave to cool slightly.
2. Add half cup sugar to the thickened milk and mix till sugar dissolves.
3. Heat the remaining sugar in a non-stick pan, on low heat, till it caramalises. Add it to the hot milk and whisk vigorously till well blended. Set aside to cool.
4. When the milk cools down to room temperature (slightly lukewarm), stir in the yogurt and mix well.
5. Set in a warm place overnight. Chill when set. Serve chilled.

   (Image on page 96)

Annexure

CHAAT MASALA
Dry-roast 4 tablespoons coriander seeds, 2 teaspoons cumin seeds and 1 teaspoon carom seeds (ajwain) separately. Cool and powder them with 2-3 whole dried red chillies, 3 tablespoons black salt and ½ teaspoon citric acid. Mix in 1 teaspoon dried mango powder (amchur), 1 tablespoon salt and 1 teaspoon white/black pepper powder. Store in an airtight container.

EGGLESS MAYONNAISE
Whisk together 2 tablespoons cream cheese and 1½ cups drained yogurt in a bowl well. Add 1 tablespoon condensed milk, salt, ½ teaspoon crushed black peppercorns and whisk again. Add 3 tablespoons olive oil, ¼ teaspoon mustard paste, ½ teaspoon lemon juice and whisk till well blended. Refrigerate the mayonnaise for an hour and use as required.

GARAM MASALA POWDER
Lightly dry-roast 10-12 blades of mace, 8-10 one-inch sticks of cinnamon, 25 cloves, 25 green cardamoms, 10-12 black cardamoms, 2 nutmegs, 8-10 bay leaves, 8 teaspoons cumin seeds, 4 teaspoons black peppercorns one by one. Cool and grind to a fine powder. (Makes 100 grams of garam masala powder)

GREEN CHUTNEY
Grind 1 cup fresh coriander leaves, ½ cup fresh mint leaves and 2-3 green chillies to a smooth paste with a little water if required. Add the black salt to taste and ¼ teaspoon sugar. Transfer the chutney into a bowl, add 1 teaspoon lemon juice, and mix well.

MANGODI
Drain 2 cups soaked skinless split green gram, grind it smoothly without water. Add ¾ teaspoon asafoetida, 1½ teaspoons ginger paste, 1½ teaspoons green chilli paste and salt and mix well. Grease 6 thali with oil. Put the ground mixture in a piping bag and press out small dumplings on the thali. You can do this using your fingers too. Sun dry the mangodi for 2-3 days or till completely dry. Cool and store them in an airtight container and use as required.

PAU BHAJI MASALA

Dry-roast 1½ tablespoons dried mango powder (amchur), 12 Kashmiri dried red chillies, ½ teaspoon black peppercorns, 2 tablespoons cumin seeds, 2½ tablespoons coriander seeds, 6 one-inch cinnamon sticks, 1 tablespoon salt, ¼ teaspoon black salt, 25 cloves, 1 black cardamom, 6-8 curry leaves, 2 bay leaves and 1 tablespoon fennel seeds (saunf) in a small non-stick pan on medium heat for 5 minutes. Cool completely and grind to a smooth powder. Store in an airtight container.

PUNJABI GARAM MASALA POWDER

One after the other dry-roast 100 grams black peppercorns, 100 grams cumin seeds, 10 grams black cardamoms, 5 cloves and 1 inch cinnamon till fragrant. Set aside to cool completely. Mix together and grind to a fine powder. Store in a dry and airtight container to use when required.

RASAM POWDER

Dry-roast 1 cup coriander seeds, ½ cup split pigeon peas, 4 tablespoons cumin seeds, 4 tablespoons black peppercorns, 12 curry leaves and 15 dried red chillies for 3-4 minutes or until fragrant. Cool and grind into a fine powder. When the powder is completely cooled, transfer into air tight jars and use as required. You can store it in a refrigerator or in cool, dry place for upto 6 months.

SWEET DATE AND TAMARIND CHUTNEY

Dry-roast 2 teaspoons cumin seeds and ¼ teaspoon fennel seeds till fragrant. Cool and grind to a powder. Mix 15-20 stoned and chopped dates with 1 cup grated jaggery, 1 cup tamarind pulp, cumin and fennel powder, 2 teaspoons red chilli powder, 1 teaspoon dried ginger powder, 1 teaspoon black salt, 1 teaspoon salt and 1 cup water in a deep non-stick pan and cook on medium heat till it comes to a boil. Reduce heat and continue to cook for 6-8 minutes or till homogenous. Cool and store in a dry bottle to use when required.

TAMARIND PULP

Soak 75 grams tamarind in 100 ml warm water for 10-15 minutes. Grind to a smooth paste and strain to remove any fibres. Store in an airtight container in the refrigerator.

VEGETABLE STOCK

Boil 5 cups of water with 1 medium sliced onion, ½ medium sliced carrot, 3 inches celery stalk, chopped, 2 garlic cloves, 1 bay leaf, 5-6 peppercorns and 2-3 cloves. Reduce the heat and simmer for 30 minutes. Strain the stock into a bowl and set aside to cool. Store in a refrigerator till further use.

Glossary

Almonds
Badam

Apple gourds
Tinde

Asafoetida
Hing

Basil seeds
Sabja/sabza/takmaria

Bay leaf
Tej patta

Beetroot
Chukandar

Black cardamoms
Badi elaichi

Black pepper powder
Kali mirch powder

Black peppercorns
Kali mirch

Black salt
Kala namak

Bottle gourd
Lauki/ghia/doodhi

Brinjal
Baingan

Butter
Makkhan

Button mushrooms
Kumbh/dhingri

Cabbage
Pattagobhi/bandgobhi

Caraway seeds
Shahi jeera

Carom leaves
Ajwain ke patte

Carom seeds
Ajwain

Carrots
Gajar

Cashew nuts
Kaju

Cauliflower
Phoolgobhi

Chickpeas
Kabuli chana

Cinnamon
Dalchini

Cloves
Laung

Cluster beans
Guar

Coconut
Nariyal

Coconut milk
Nariyal ka doodh

Coconut oil
Nariyal ka tel

Colocasia leaves
Arbi ke patte

Coriander powder
Dhania powder

Coriander seeds
Sabut dhania

Corn niblets/kernels
Makai ke dane

Cottage cheese
Paneer

Crushed black peppercorns
Kuti kali mirch

Cucumber
Kakdi/Kheera

Cumin powder
Jeera powder

Cumin seeds
Jeera

Curry leaves
Kadi patta/meetha neem

Dates
Khajur

Dried fenugreek leaves
Kasoori methi

Dried mango powder
Amchur

Dried pomegranate seeds
Anardane

Dried red chillies
Sookhi lal mirch

Drumsticks
Saijan ki phalli

Fennel powder
Saunf powder

Fennel seeds
Saunf

Fenugreek seeds
Methi dana

Field beans
Dalimbi

French beans
Farsi

Fresh coriander leaves
Hara dhania

Fresh coriander stems
Hara dhania ke danthal

Fresh cream
Malai

Fresh fenugreek leaves
Methi

Fresh mint leaves
Pudina

Fesh pomegranate kernels
Taze anar ke dane

Fresh spinach leaves
Palak

Gamboge
Kokum

Ginger
Adrak

Ginger paste
Adrak ka paste

Gram flour
Besan

Green capsicum
Hari Shimla mirch

Green cardamoms
Chhoti elaichi

English	Hindi	English	Hindi	English	Hindi

Green cardamom powder
Chhoti elaichi powder
Green chillies
Hari mirch
Green chilli paste
Hari mirch ka paste
Green gram dumplings
Mangodi
Green peas
Matar
Honey
Shahad/madhu
Horse gram
Koolith
Indian gooseberry
Amla
Jackfruit
Kathal
Jaggery
Gur
Kidney beans
Rajma
Ladies' finger
Bhindi
Lemon juice
Nimboo ka ras
Lettuce leaves
Salad ke patte
Lotus stem
Bhein/kamal kakdi
Mace
Javitri
Mawa/khoya
Unsweetened condensed milk
Mustard oil
Rai ka tel/sarson ka tel
Mustard seeds
Rai/sarson
Nutmeg powder
Jaiphal powder
Peach
Adu
Peanuts/ground nuts
Moongphali
Pistachio
Pista
Poppy seeds
Khus khus

Potatoes
Aloo
Powdered sugar
Pisi hui cheeni
Pressed rice
Poha
Pure ghee
Desi ghee
Raisins
Kishmish
Red chilli powder
Lal mirch powder
Red pumpkin
Kaddu
Refined flour
Maida
Rice
Chawal
Rice flour
Chawal ka atta
Ridge gourd
Turai
Roasted Bengal gram
Daalia
Roasted cumin powder
Bhuna jeera powder
Roasted peanuts
Bhuni moongphali
Rose water
Gulab jal
Saffron
Kesar
Salt
Namak
Screw pine water
Kewra jal
Semolina
Rawa/sooji
Sesame
Til
Skinless split black gram
Dhuli urad dal
Skinless split green gram
Dhuli moong dal
Split Bengal gram
Chana dal

Split pigeon peas
Toovar dal/arhar dal
Star anise
Phool chakri/badiyan
Sugar
Cheeni/shakkar
Sugar crystals
Khadi sakhar/mishri
Sweet date and tamarind chutney
Khajur aur imli ki meethi chutney
Tamarind pulp
Imli ka guda
Tea leaves
Chai ke patte
Tomatoes
Tamatar
Tomato purée
Peesa hua tamatar
Turmeric powder
Haldi powder
Turnip
Shalgam
Unripe banana
Kachcha kela
Unripe mango
Keri
Unripe papaya
Kachcha papita
Vinegar
Sirka
Water chestnut flour
Singhare ka atta
Watermelon
Tarbooj
White sesame seeds
Safed til
Whole Black gram
Sabut urad
Whole green gram
Sabut moong
Whole red lentils
Sabut masoor
Whole-wheat flour
Gehun ka atta
Yellow dried peas
Sookhe matar
Yogurt
Dahi

Measurements

Ingredients	Quantity	Weight	Ingredients	Quantity	Weight
Almonds	10	15 grams	Curry leaves	10	1 gram
Asafoetida (hing)	1 teaspoon	4 grams	Dried fenugreek leaves		
Baking powder	1 teaspoon	3 grams	(kasoori methi)	1 tablespoon	1 gram
Baking soda (soda bicarbonate)	1 teaspoon	4 grams	Dried mango powder (amchur)	1 teaspoon	1 gram
Basmati rice	1 cup	200 grams	Dried pomegranate seeds		
Bay leaf	1	0.5 gram	(anardane)	1 teaspoon	3 grams
Beetroot, medium	1	145 grams	Dried red chillies	10	20 grams
Black cardamoms	11	10 grams	Dried white peas	1¼ cups	250 grams
Black pepper powder	1 teaspoon	3 grams	Fennel seeds (saunf)	1 teaspoon	3 grsms
Black peppercorns	5	1 gram	Fennel seeds (saunf)	1 tablespoon	9 grams
Black salt	1 teaspoon	5 grams	Fennel seeds (saunf) powder	1 teaspoon	3 grams
Boondi	1 tablespoon	7 grams	Fenugreek leaves	1 cup chopped	40 grams
Bottle gourd	1 small	250 grams	Fenugreek seeds (methi dane)	1 teaspoon	5 grams
Breadcrumbs	1 cup	110 grams	French beans	10	75 grams
Brinjal, medium	1	30 grams	Fresh button mushrooms	10 medium	125 grams
Butter	1 tablespoon	15 grams	Fresh coriander leaves	1 small bunch	150 grams
Butter	1 cup	150 grams	Fresh coriander leaves	1 medium bunch	250 grams
Button mushrooms	10 medium	125 grams	Fresh cream	1 cup	200 ml
Cabbage medium	1	650 grams	Fresh cream	4 tablespoons	60 ml
Caraway seeds (shahi jeera)	1 teaspoon	3 grams	Fresh fenugreek leaves	1 small bunch	175 grams
Carom seeds (ajwain)	1 teaspoon	2 grams	Fresh fenugreek leaves	1 medium bunch	250 grams
Carrot, medium	1	90 grams	Fresh fenugreek leaves	1 large bunch	580 grams
Cashew nut paste	1 cup	225 grams	Fresh green peas (shelled)	1 cup	150 gms
Cashew nuts	10	20 grams	Fresh mint leaves	1 medium bunch	85 grams
Cauliflower medium	1	500 grams	Fresh mint leaves	1 large bunch	110 grams
Chaat masala	1 teaspoon	1 gm	Fresh mint leaves	1 small bunch	60 grams
Chickpeas	½ cup	100 grams	Fresh pomegranate kernels	1 cup	180 grams
Chopped dates	1 cup	175 grams	Fresh pomegranate kernels	1 tablespoon	10 grams
Cinnamon	1 inch/2.5 cm stick	0.5 gram	Fresh spinach leaves	1 small bunch	150 grams
Cinnamon powder	1 tsp	2 grams	Fresh spinach leaves	1 medium bunch	250 grams
Cloves	10	1 gm	Fresh spinach leaves	1 large bunch	450 grams
Coconut, freshly grated	1 cup	110 grams	Fresh tomato puree	1 cup	235 grams
Coconut milk	1 cup	200 ml	Ginger	½ inch	5 grams
Coriander powder	1 teaspoon	2 grams	Ginger	1 inch	10 grams
Coriander powder	1 tablespoon	6 grams	Ginger paste	1 tablespoon	15 grams
Coriander seeds	1 teaspoon	2 grams	Gram flour (besan)	1 cup	100 gms
Coriander seeds	1 tablespoon	6 grams	Green capsicum, medium	1	110 grams
Corn kernels	1 cup	150 grams	Green capsicum, large	1	180 grams
Cornflour	1 tablespoon	5 grams	Green capsicum, small	1	60 grams
Cottage cheese (paneer), grated	½ cup	70 grams	Green cardamom powder	1 teaspoon	2 grams
Cucumber, medium	1	125 grams	Green cardamoms	10	3 grams
Cucumber, small	1	75 grams	Green chilli	1	2 grams
Cumin powder	1 teaspoon	3 grams	Green chilli paste	1 teaspoon	5 grams
Cumin seeds	1 tablespoon	9 grams	Green chutney	2 tablespoons	27 grams
Cumin seeds (jeera)	¾ cup + 1 tbsp	100 grams	Green chutney	¼ cup	48 grams

Ingredients	Quantity	Weight	Ingredients	Quantity	Weight
Honey	1 tablespoon	15 ml	Rose syrup	1 tablespoon	15 ml
Indian gooseberry (amla)	1	35 grams	Salt	1 teaspoon	5 grams
Jaggery, grated	1 cup	200 grams	Semolina	1 cup	200 grams
Jaggery, grated	1 teaspoon	10 grams	Semolina (rawa/suji)	1 tablespoon	13 grams
Jaggery, grated	1 tablespoon	30 grams	Singhare ka atta		
Karela, large	1	110 grams	(water chestnut flour)	1 tablespoon	10 grams
Karela, medium	1	75 grams	Spinach leaves	1 medium bunch	250 grams
Karela, small	1	30 grams	Spinach leaves	1 small bunch	150 grams
Kokum petals	1 cup	100 grams	Spinach leaves	1 large bunch	350 grams
Kokum petals	10	15 grams	Split Bengal gram (chana dal)	1 cup	200 grams
Kokum sherbet	6 tbsps	80 ml	Split Bengal gram (chana dal)	1 teaspoon	5 grams
Ladies' fingers	40 medium	300 grams	Split skinless black gram		
Lemon juice	1 tablespoon	15 ml	(dhuli urad dal)	½ cup	100 grams
Lemon juice	1 teaspoon	5 ml	Split skinless black gram		
Mace (javitri)	2 blades	3 grams	(dhuli urad dal)	1 tablespoon	15 grams
Mawa/khoya, grated	1 cup	180 grams	Split black gram with skin		
Mawa/khoya, grated	1 tablespoon	20 grams	(chilkewali urad dal)	½ cup	100 grams
Milk	1 cup	200 ml	Split black gram with skin		
Mustard seeds	1 tablespoon	10 grams	(chilkewali urad dal)	1 cup	200 grams
Mustard seeds	1 teaspoon	4 grams	Split lentils (masoor dal)	1 cup	200 grams
Nutmeg powder	1 teaspoon	0.5 gram	Split pigeon pea (toor dal/arhar dal)	1 cup	200 grams
Oil	1 tablespoon	15 ml	Split red lentils (masoor dal)	1 cup	200 grams
Peanuts	1 tablespoon	10 grams	Split skinless black gram		
Peanuts	1 cup	200 grams	(dhuli urad dal)	1 teaspoon	5 grams
Pistachios	20	10 grams	Split skinless green gram		
Pistachios	¼ cup	30 grams	(dhuli moong dal)	1 cup	200 grams
Pomegranate seeds (anardana)	1 teaspoon	3 grams	Star anise	1	2 grams
Poppy seeds (khus khus)	1 tablespoon	12 grams	Sugar	1 tablespoon	15 grams
Poppy seeds (khus khus)	1 teaspoon	4 grams	Sugar	1 cup	250 grams
Potato, large	1	150 grams	Sugar	1 teaspoon	5 grams
Potato, medium	1	100 grams	Sweet date and tamarind chutney	¼ cup	60 grams
Powdered sugar	1 tablespoon	8 grams	Tamarind pulp	1 teaspoon	5 grams
Powdered sugar	1 cup	125 grams	Tamarind pulp	1 tablespoon	20 grams
Pure ghee/desi ghee	1 cup	180 grams	Tomato puree, fresh	1 tablespoon	15 grams
Raisins (white, black)	1 tablespoon	10 grams	Tomato, large	1	110 grams
Raisins (white, black)	1 tsp	5 grams	Tomato, medium	1	95 grams
Raisins (white, black)	10	5 grams	Tomato, small	1	60 grams
Raisins (white, black)	½ cup	90 grams	Turmeric powder (haldi)	1 tablespoon	9 grams
Red chilli powder	1 tablespoon	10 grams	Turmeric powder (haldi)	1 teaspoon	3 grams
Red chilli powder	1 teaspoon	3 grams	Unripe bananas, medium	4	440 grams
Red kidney beans (rajma)	1 cup	200 grams	Unripe mango, large	1	300 grams
Refined flour (maida)	1 cup	120 grams	Unripe mango, medium	1	125 grams
Refined flour (maida)	2 tablespoons	15 grams	Unripe mango, small	1	80 grams
Rice	1 cup	200 grams	Unripe mango	1 small	100 grams
Rice, beaten	1 cup	117 grams	Vinegar	1 tablespoon	15 ml
Rice flour	1 cup	150 grams	White sesame seeds	1 cup	160 grams
Rice flour	1 teaspoon	4 grams	Whole black gram (sabut urad)	1 cup	250 grams
Ripe mango, small	6	900 grams	Whole green gram (sabut moong)	1 cup	240 grams
Roasted chana dal (daalia)	1 cup	130 grams	Whole wheat flour (gehun ka atta)	1 cup	150 grams
Roasted cumin powder	1 tablespoon	9 grams	Yellow capsicum, large	1	180 grams
Roasted cumin powder	1 teaspoon	3 grams	Yellow capsicum, medium	1	110 grams
Roasted peanuts	2 tablespoons	15 grams	Yellow capsicum, small	1	60 grams
Roasted peanuts	¼ cup	30 grams	Yogurt	1 cup	250 grams